Radical OBM

Organizational Behavior Management
for Regular Folks

Portia James, M.A., BCBA

Acknowledgments:

First, I am grateful to God for bestowing upon me a compelling and relatable narrative rooted in experiences that only His guidance could have led me through.

To my husband who encourages me to say 'yes' to anything that my creative mind can fathom.

To my mother, a first-generation businesswoman, who instilled in me the wisdom to understand the freedom of letting go.

To my sisters - Jayda, Chanavian, and Tasia - who remind me daily of my humanity and power. Y'all are otherworldly, and I learn from you all every day.

To Peter Jackson, my very first business coach, who granted me the permission to concentrate on what truly counts and introduced me to Nas' *"I'm on Fire"* - the theme song of this season of my life.

To Adrienne Bradley, who encouraged me to write this curriculum the first time we ever spoke. Thank you for making it your mission to amplify black voices and create black spaces.

And to My Readers -
If you discover any essence or nuanced essence of yourself in this book, I felt from the bottom of my heart that you deserved to be acknowledged.

Whether that's a good or a bad thing is a reflection of you.

Contents.

Preface.

What would YOU do if you finally had a seat at the table — but didn't have permission to speak? *That was me.*

I had worked my whole life for that seat... one where I was always trying to prove my worth. I published my first written work at the age of 10. Finished high school with an above-average GPA, graduated college Cum Laude, immediately landed a great job, moved up the ranks, self-published seven books, checked every box and then some. I didn't realize it then, but I was doing everything in my power to NOT become a statistic - because before I was even born... I was supposed to be one.

My Mom got pregnant at 14. My grandparents were addicts. Society told us that 'WE' would never amount to anything. I needed to prove society wrong. I'm still working on that. To backtrack for a second, I'm going to paint a picture for you: imagine a little girl, a stepchild, desperately wanting to fit in at home and in school. *That was also me.*

My parents moved us from Pomona, California, just down the way to Fontana, for a chance to attend better school districts. As one of the few black kids at my school, I stood out and so badly wanted to blend in. *To belong.* My way of being accepted was to never give anyone a reason to doubt me. So I performed. I excelled - I did that all throughout school, and yes - I even did it in the corporate world.

Fast-forward... There I was - at my dream job - the only Director of Clinical Operations at a nationally well-known Behavioral Treatment company where I was helping children and families with autism. I ensured that children in marginalized communities had representation in their homes, schools, and communities. *I was making a difference.* I ensured that children and their families had the tools they needed and that they FELT LIKE THEY BELONGED. Yet, I still didn't feel like I did.

Once again, I was an 'Only' - the only woman in most rooms, certainly the only woman of color in those rooms. So, I made myself small. And then, one day, I spoke up. Why? I discovered that my male colleague (with fewer qualifications) was making $60,000 more than I was. Guess what happened? I was fired immediately. Broken... and sadly, a statistic. With essentially zero self-confidence left and no real sense of direction after having dedicated half my life to this industry, I couldn't bring myself to get back into corporate America and give them another opportunity to destroy me. So, I started my own company... actually companies - with a mission to ensure everyone has a fair shot — a fair chance.

LET'S START WITH COMPANY #1 — Behavior Genius®

In my years of experience, I've seen that children of color are diagnosed with autism an average of 3 years later than children who are not diverse. But early intervention is essential to ensuring the best possible outcomes for children. Children of color deserve equal access to quality behavior treatment. It is no longer acceptable for us to ignore the call to action. And this is why I built Behavior Genius®. ABA companies have a responsibility to hire diverse team members who can provide education and resources to all children, including those in marginalized communities.

ABA was designed in a way that centers the "elite." The parents who can afford the best insurance. The ones who can survive on one parent's income while the other stays at home to attend daily therapy sessions with their child - *if there are two*. But that's not the reality for the population that I serve. Or of my own upbringing.

But why have one business when you can have two? Yep - Still overachieving. But it's not about me. It's about what I've seen and who I serve. Did you know that 80% of black-owned businesses fail within the first 18 months? *But they don't have to.* Genius Operations® is the first Operations company curated for, and committed to, the advancement of black behavior analysts.

Black professionals have substantially lower access to the resources needed to build and maintain sustainable companies. This is especially true in ABA, where only 3.9% of all Behavior Analysts are black. This lack of resources can be credited to a lack of business operations training and diminished opportunities to advance in the workplace.

At Genius Operations®, we know that if we give minority clinician-owned companies the tools they need to thrive, they will do it with flying colors. And those children in unseen communities will have access to the same quality of care as everyone else. Little black and brown girls like me will grow up and *know* they belong.

One thing about those tables - they turn. In the end, those tables - the ones I wanted a seat at so badly - weren't the ones I was supposed to be at. I built my own table - but not just for me... for everyone who has ever felt like they didn't have a seat. That's the legacy I'm working relentlessly to leave behind. That's the *only* table I want to sit at.

Don't you?

Chapter 1:
Radical OBM

"Can't we just throw some balls in the air and see where they land?"

I will never forget the day my CEO posed the most bizarre question to the entire Leadership Team. And by the looks on everyone else's faces, I knew I wasn't the only one who thought it was a joke. Granted, this woman was not a Behavior Analyst; however, she was an executive powerhouse (or so I thought), and honestly, I expected more from her for that reason alone. I had been certified in Organizational Behavior Management for several years; However, it was her type of leadership, critical thinking, and problem-solving skills (or lack thereof) that ignited my love for Operations. I didn't understand how she had gotten as far up as she had without believing wholeheartedly in strategy or people. Still, I became determined to show her that systems worked. And not only that, but I could use everything I knew about Human Behavior to rock the company's core for the better. Needless to say, she wasn't the least bit interested in my take on Operational Efficiency. In fact, I'm pretty sure she resented my entire existence. Who did I think I was anyway, using science and common human decency to find sustainable solutions to her multi-million dollar problems? Four out of five times, though, I had the right idea and the data to prove it.

The origins of OBM can be traced back to the early 1900s when Frederick Taylor developed his scientific management approach. Taylor believed that scientific methods could be used to increase productivity by improving the efficiency of work processes. His practice focused on analyzing tasks and breaking them into component parts, which could then be optimized for maximum efficiency. Sound familiar? That's because it is! Behavior Analysts use Task Analyses to break down large tasks into their parts. Doing this lets us pinpoint areas of concern and provide intervention in one step rather than looking at the entire task. At the organizational level, Behavior Analysts and business leaders can take a microscope to each process within the organization and minimize it to its minor parts. We are allowed to be caught up in the details, explore what's beneath the surface, and find solutions to problems that the average person may not even know exist.

In the 1930s, Elton Mayo conducted the famous Hawthorne studies, which focused on the effects of environmental factors on worker productivity. This research helped to establish the importance of social factors in organizational behavior and the need to consider employee motivation and morale. Now, we're talkin'! If you know anything about setting events and antecedents, then you know what this is all about. This was when the field realized that *people* were at the core of every organization. And people, although complex, can be quite predictable if we view them as a product of their environment. From there, it is our life's work as OBM Specialists to analyze how the environment impacts the people inside of it and how we impact the environment around us. This is the basis of individual work ethic and collective culture - two dependent variables that can be designed, taught, and managed using Organizational Behavior Management.

The 1950s saw the emergence of B.F. Skinner's behaviorism - Alas, a name we all know and love. Skinner emphasized the importance of environmental factors in shaping behavior. Skinner's work on operant conditioning provided a framework for understanding how rewards and punishments can be used to shape behavior in the workplace. Imagine that!

In the 1960s, OBM began to take shape as a distinct field of study, with the founding of the Journal of Applied Behavior Analysis and the establishment of the Association for Behavior Analysis. During this time, OBM researchers began to develop methods for applying behavioral principles to organizational settings, including performance management, feedback, and goal-setting.

In the 1980s and 1990s (shoutout to 80's babies everywhere), OBM continued to evolve, emphasizing the importance of organizational culture and leadership in shaping behavior. Researchers began to explore the role of communication, collaboration, and teamwork in promoting organizational effectiveness.

Today, OBM is used across various industries, including healthcare, education, and manufacturing. Businesses use OBM to improve employee performance, reduce turnover, and increase productivity - three critical factors to the development and thrivorship of an ABA Company. In the medical industry, OBM improves patient safety and reduces medical errors. In education, OBM enhances student performance and promotes positive behavior.

While OBM has made significant strides in improving organizational performance, much work still needs to be done to promote diversity, equity, and inclusion in the field. Research has shown that women and people of color are underrepresented in leadership positions in OBM, and there is a need for greater diversity and inclusion in the field. Additionally, research (or lack thereof) suggests a need for greater attention to social justice and equity issues in OBM research and practice.

The lack of attention or genuine interest in DEI uniquely impacts the Autism industry. The Behavior Analyst Certification Board Code of Ethics (2022 version, 1.07) clearly states that Behavior Analysts should actively engage in professional development activities to acquire knowledge and skills related to cultural responsiveness and diversity. It even discusses the critical evaluation of our own biases and ability to address the needs of individuals with diverse backgrounds, including those we supervise. However, marginalized populations are still underrepresented at the leadership level and even more so at the operational and executive levels. This means that people at the top make decisions for people of color without a clear, intentional understanding of our unique needs. It also means that those decisions often exclude entire communities where ABA services are most needed *(see Systemic Racism)*. And although some people will spend the rest of their days trying to convince us, and themselves, that it has nothing to do with race, according to the National Library of Medicine, "Racism is considered a fundamental cause of adverse health outcomes for racial/ethnic minorities and racial/ethnic inequities in health."

If you are in the service industry, you were likely led here by your innate love for helping people. If you've been in the game as long as I have, perhaps your reach has extended out to hundreds of children and their families directly and indirectly through the people you have developed along the way. Bravo to you! But there's always more work to be done. At the Organizational Level, we have the power, and the responsibility, to leverage a 120-year-old science - one that was never designed with people of color in mind - to build companies that serve to close the gap in access to behavioral healthcare for individual recipients of Behavior Analytic services.

This course intends to shift your perspective and (if I've served you well) maybe even the views of those around you. I know firsthand that if this course can shift your perspective, it will also have the power to uplevel your work, your organization, and the communities you serve. This isn't about mindset; it's about having a better *vantage point.*

I have a natural admiration for words and how we can use them to send hidden messages. Take "Radical," for example. Although it sounds cool, I even chose the title of this course intentionally.

→ Relating to or affecting the fundamental nature of something

→ Far-reaching or thorough

→ Advocating or based on thorough or complete political or social change

I often reflect on that story from earlier - Every time I encounter a problem to work through or feel especially attacked by an operational landmine! And also, admittedly, when I am discouraged. I think back to all the people I had the opportunity to impact under poor leadership - a type of dictatorship that didn't give two fucks about the people in the back. And I am reminded of my power from *this* vantage point. I know what it's like to feel powerless. And I also know that if people who look and think like me never develop the courage to rise to the top and build companies that stand the test of time and turnover, our reach will never extend beyond our comfort zones. I knew that day that I had an even broader mission to fulfill; *a mission for REFORM.*

After all, a wise older white woman at an Autism conference once told me, "Skinner is dead. Why are we still taking advice from an old, dead, white guy?" This is an unpopular opinion that I had never thought of in that way before, but I do now.

Systemic Racism is a pervasive and deeply ingrained societal pattern or structure that systematically disadvantages certain racial or ethnic groups. It is a form of discrimination built into institutions, policies, and practices, leading to unequal opportunities, outcomes, and experiences for different racial groups.

Chapter 2:
Radical Values

There is no conversation about leadership without talking extensively about burnout. And for the sake of Radical Conversation, here's an unpopular opinion: *Burnout is a choice.* Triggered? Hear me out.

The COVID-19 pandemic brought the dawn of a new wave of cultural norms in the workplace. People who once felt entitled now feel even more entitled than ever. People who battle anxiety have even more reasons to be anxious. People who were once focused are now constantly distracted. Those who have always been resourceful are now crippled by their own learned helplessness. The list goes on. There is a clear separation between generations that thickens the air in workplaces across the globe. There is a call for unconditional emotional safety in the workplace with little to no regard for the unconditional work ethic that was instilled in our great-grandparents.

As leaders, these are the waters that we are navigating. While it's easy to lose focus by attempting to meet the demands of our team, it is also essential that we constantly remind ourselves of what matters most to *us* and to let our personal values be what guides our professional decisions and actions. By staying wildly authentic and committed to the things that light us up and set us on fire, we pave the way for better outcomes for our clients and our teams by fostering relationships based on trust, understanding of the human condition, and the collective well-being of everyone involved.

Burnout, especially in our industry and *especially* for black people, stems from two core places: Compassion Fatigue and The Invisible Workload.

Compassion fatigue refers to the emotional exhaustion and diminished empathy experienced by individuals who regularly care for others, particularly in high-stress professions such as healthcare or social work. It arises from the constant exposure to others' suffering, leading to a depletion of one's emotional resources and a reduced ability to provide empathetic care. This is why the idea of "leading with empathy" is difficult for most people in leadership positions; however, in the service industry, leading with empathy is paramount to the success of everyone involved.

The invisible workload refers to the often unacknowledged or unrecognized tasks and responsibilities that disproportionately fall on individuals - especially black women - in addition to their formal job roles.

This additional burden can have a significant impact on women in several ways:

1. Emotional labor: Black women may experience an increased expectation to manage and regulate emotions within their professional roles and personal interactions. We are expected to navigate racial and gender biases and stereotypes while presenting ourselves as confident, approachable, and non-threatening. This emotional labor is exhausting and often contributes to added stress and burnout.

2. Mentorship and sponsorship gaps: Black women often face limited access to mentorship and sponsorship opportunities within organizations. We may have to invest additional effort in seeking mentors who understand our unique experiences and can provide guidance and support.

3. Diversity and inclusion work: Black women often carry the burden of advocating for diversity and inclusion within our organizations. We may take on extra responsibilities such as participating in diversity committees, mentoring other minority employees, or being the representative for underrepresented groups. These efforts, while important, can add to the workload and distract from our core job responsibilities.

4. Code-switching and navigating biases: In many work environments, black professionals face biases and microaggressions that require us to code-switch, altering their communication style, appearance, or behavior (typically all of the above) to conform to the dominant culture. This constant navigation of biases and the pressure to adapt is mentally and

emotionally draining. Code-switching is a trauma response that requires us to betray ourselves daily to protect our emotional safety in the workplace.

5. Intersectionality: Black women face the intersection of gender and racial biases, which can exacerbate the invisible workload we already experience. We encounter unique challenges that stem from the combined effects of racism and sexism, leading to a more significant impact on our career progression, opportunities for advancement, and overall well-being.

And I didn't forget about the brothers. The invisible workload also impacts black men in various ways, although their experiences may differ from those of black women. Here are some ways in which the invisible workload can affect black men:

1. Stereotype threat and performance pressure: Black men often face the burden of disproving negative stereotypes and navigating expectations associated with their race. They may feel the pressure to perform exceptionally well to counteract biases and assumptions. This additional mental and emotional load can impact their well-being and job performance.

Short Story: A team member had been working for me for several years. She was recently promoted to a new role with the primary objective of ensuring smooth operations at our treatment center. Despite possessing all the necessary skills, qualifications, and capabilities to handle the position effortlessly, she quickly became overwhelmed and began expressing her distress to her managers and peers.

Curious about the source of her overwhelm, I inquired further and asked why she had taken on additional tasks unrelated to her job's expectations. She confided in me that she felt compelled to assume extra responsibilities due to our company being black-owned. She believed it was necessary to prove anyone with negative opinions about us wrong. The weight of countering stereotypes made her think we constantly had to present ourselves as 100 times better than any other company.

While I sincerely appreciated her sense of responsibility and commitment to combating the invisible truths that had plagued me personally since our company's inception, I was also dismayed by the realization that people of color within my organization still felt compelled, perhaps more than anywhere else, to overextend themselves. This realization troubled me, as it highlighted the enduring need for people of color to go above and beyond.

Regrettably, her efforts to prove our worthiness inadvertently led to poor performance in critical areas of her work. Additionally, she unintentionally perpetuated the "hustle culture" that I had tirelessly endeavored to dismantle within our organization. Moreover, she shared her concerns with others, which had a detrimental impact on our organizational culture. Ultimately, the mounting pressure became too much for her, and she made the difficult decision to resign, leaving behind a team that greatly admired her while also burdening them with rectifying the aftermath of her departure.

2. Leadership expectations: Black men may face unique expectations and pressures regarding leadership roles. They may be perceived as natural leaders or held to higher standards of competence and assertiveness. This can result in added responsibilities and the need to constantly prove themselves, contributing to higher stress levels.

3. Mentorship and representation: Like black women, black men may encounter challenges accessing mentorship and finding role models within their organizations. The lack of representation and limited opportunities for guidance can place the onus on them to seek out mentors who can understand their experiences and provide support.

4. Navigating bias and discrimination: Black men may face biases, stereotypes, and discriminatory practices in the workplace. They may need to navigate these challenges while managing their own emotional responses, which can be emotionally draining even on the best days.

5. Intersectionality: Black men also experience intersectionality, where the combined effects of racism and other intersecting identities, such as gender or sexual orientation, can compound their experiences of the invisible workload. For example, a black man who presents with a disability may

encounter heightened challenges and societal expectations that intersect with both race and neurodiversity.

And let's not overlook the impact of **weaponized incompetence** on our workloads. As leaders, we are all too familiar with individuals we manage, and even those who manage us, attempting to evade accountability by making us the bottleneck in decision-making rather than employing their resources and taking responsibility for their actions and choices.

Organizations must recognize and address the invisible workload that affects black professionals. This involves creating inclusive environments, providing opportunities for mentorship and advancement, actively managing bias and discrimination, and creating support systems that acknowledge and alleviate the additional burdens black people face in the workplace. Organizations can foster a more equitable and supportive workplace for black professionals and other underrepresented groups by recognizing and easing the invisible workload.

But What Can We Control Now?

Jamie Varon said, "The distance between what you love and what you do will be the size of your unhappiness." The number one cause of burnout in every area of life is a misalignment in values. On a macro level, we should continuously assess whether or not the values of the company we work for align with our personal values. On a micro level, leaders should regularly evaluate the role of our own values in how we show up for the people we serve. The number one indicator that these misalignments exist is toxic workplace behavior (i.e., gossip, complaining, refusal to problem-solve, lack of accountability, failure to thrive, etc.). Toxic workplace behavior leads to burnout not only of the individual person but of the people around them. When we stay focused on our unique contributions, we create a powerful connection that circles back to the values of our consumers. This is why we must resist the urge to entertain distractions and stay intentionally and unconditionally aligned with our personal values. This is how we can make our highest contribution without sacrificing our sanity.

In this chapter, I will use a few of my core values as examples of how our personal values shape us as professionals, leaders, and humans.

Value 1 - The Wow-Factor

Like almost every black woman I know, I was taught from an early age to always be the exception. People of color are often underestimated. In fact, the higher up we go in our careers, our intrinsic need for belonging forces us to conform to the social pressures of being sensational. I would even go as far as to say that, especially for black women, our emotional safety, job security, and opportunities for advancement all rely heavily on our ability to impress others into believing that we are worthy. This fundamental truth is why I built my work ethic around getting people to recognize that I could do the work and would make it my mission to show parents that their child was also capable of surpassing their expectations and blowing their minds.

For illustration, I'm going to ask you a question: *How quickly after purchasing a product do you expect that product to work?* If you twisted your face up and mumbled, *"immediately,"* you just offered the perfect segway to my next point: your clients want to know whether or not the science that you love and that you have invested your time, effort, and money into - the science that their doctor sold them - works. And they want to know immediately. Parents of children with special needs have experienced perpetual frustration. They have lost hope. And ABA services will inconvenience them whether or not it works. So they need to know the value of their investment in the same way you need to know if your new iPhone works before leaving the store.

Some clinicians would fold under that type of pressure. But what parents have to offer just in the fact that they are choosing ABA is their willingness to try again. And what we have to give in return is an opportunity to make it worth it for them. We have an obligation to think outside the box and ask questions that will guide our treatment in a way that brings about a mother's happy tears and a father's grateful embrace at the end of our time with every family we serve. Right from the beginning, before imposing the principles of Behavior Analysis onto our families, we should be asking our clients and/or their parents two questions that will give us an immediate understanding of what they need most:

→   What are 3 things that would change your life?

→   What is most critical for you at this time?

From there, it is vital that whatever response they provide is honored in the design of their child's program and that progress toward the things that they value is evident as early on in their child's treatment as possible. This is how you become unforgettable. Because guess what - nobody else even cared to ask. Immediately, whether or not they underestimate you, you now have their undivided attention. And what is most remarkable is that when you pair their need for a small miracle with your determination to surpass their expectations, you now have a shared interest and clarity of purpose that serves your client, their family, and yourself.

Value 2 - Holistic Care

I am family-oriented. I declared a major in psychology during my first year in college. I went straight to graduate school, where I funneled my love for marriage and family therapy into a career in Behavior Analysis. Pinpointing my career path was easy. During my undergraduate internship, I realized that ABA gave me the best possible vantage point for helping families: from right inside their homes. To quote Maya Angelou, "Your legacy is every life you touch." Science is often narrow-minded, and so are its people. But what would happen if we were to stretch our hearts and minds toward an approach to treatment that dares to recognize the needs of the child and the ecosystem around that child?

The challenges and effects of raising a child with special needs often extend beyond the individual and affect parents, siblings, and extended family members. Here are some common ways in which families are impacted:

Emotional impact: Raising a child with autism can bring about a range of emotions for parents and family members. Initially, there may be feelings of confusion, grief, or shock upon receiving the diagnosis. Ongoing challenges related to communication difficulties, behavioral issues, and the need for specialized care can lead to stress, frustration, and isolation.

Financial impact: Autism can place a considerable financial strain on families. The costs associated with therapy, interventions, medical care, and specialized education can be substantial. Additionally, some families may face increased medical expenses and the need for additional support services for their children and themselves.

Time and energy commitment: Children with autism often require significant time and attention. Parents may need to dedicate extensive hours to attending therapy sessions, doctor's appointments, and individualized education program (IEP) meetings. This can result in limited personal time, reduced work hours, or the need for one parent to stay home, affecting the family's overall dynamics.

Sibling dynamics: Siblings of children with autism often experience their own unique challenges. They might have to adapt to changes in family routines and dynamics and cope with the emotional and behavioral challenges their sibling with autism may present. Siblings may also require additional support and attention to address any feelings of neglect or resentment that may arise.

Social isolation: Families with a child on the autism spectrum may face social isolation due to the challenges of participating in typical family activities. Parents may encounter difficulties finding suitable childcare options or arranging playdates and outings with other families. This isolation can impact the overall well-being of both parents and siblings.

Marital and parental stress: When I first entered the field, the average divorce rate for parents of children with autism was 83% - imagine how much higher that number may have been for people of color who already face higher-the-average divorce rates. The stressors associated with raising a child with autism can strain marriages and parenting dynamics. The constant demands, emotional challenges, and differing opinions on treatment approaches can lead to increased conflict and stress between parents. It is essential for couples to communicate openly, seek support, and engage in self-care to help maintain a healthy relationship. It is also important that ABA providers recognize this need and work to resolve conflict by establishing effective behavior support plans and gaining buy-in from both parents (and step-parents whenever possible).

Extended family support: Extended family members, such as grandparents, aunts, and uncles, may also be impacted by a child with autism. They may support and assist the immediate family, contribute financially, or help care for the child. However, extended family members may also face challenges in understanding and accepting autism, which can create additional stress within the family unit.

It is worth noting that the impact on families can vary significantly depending on the severity of the child's needs, available support services, and the resources and resilience of the family. Seeking early intervention, accessing support groups, and utilizing community resources can help families better navigate the challenges associated with autism and promote the overall well-being of all family members.

As clinicians, we can do our part by understanding the individual and collective needs of our clients' families. For example, instead of asking the question, "How are you?" at the beginning of every session, try diving just a little deeper:

→ How are you *feeling* about toilet training?

→ How are you *coping* with your child's emotional outbursts?

→ How are you *sleeping* at night?

→ How are you *balancing/juggling* your child's therapies?

When providing a therapeutic service, the most well-rounded clinicians consider how the family is impacted not only by the child but also by the presence or absence of the service itself. It is also important to acknowledge what is underlying or playing in the background for the family, what unspoken challenges the parents face, and what factors may hinder their ability to actively participate in their child's treatment. Once you have the answers to these questions based on your observations and/or asking clarifying questions, you have all you need to design client programs that address family dynamics that may impact the child's clinical outcomes.

Value 3 - Focused Care

Providing quality care for any service type necessitates identifying and understanding the pain points experienced by the individuals being served. The critical question to answer is: What problem are you solving? However, it is equally important to recognize the issues that you are not solving. For instance, you are not curing autism, and it is not likely that you will change the child's natural inclinations or way of being.

To maintain focus, it is crucial to acknowledge each caregiver's vision for their child, themselves, and their family. For example, a family's goal might be for their child to participate in a sports team or be integrated into a general education classroom. It could be as simple as enabling the child to independently complete a morning or evening routine, allowing the caregivers to attend to a younger sibling. Another goal might involve creating opportunities for the family to spend quality time together in various settings, with autism not interfering.

Unfortunately, people often become more preoccupied with immediate concerns rather than the desired long-term outcomes for the family. Behavior analysts, for instance, may find themselves overly focused on numerous minor issues instead of addressing the two or three critical aspects that truly matter. However, when we are consumed by everything, we end up being focused on nothing at all. This explains why, despite working tirelessly, clinicians may feel burnt out while their clients fail to make the progress they could achieve. By staying attuned to the needs and desires of the family and aligning the program accordingly, clinicians can become valuable assets not only to the organization but also to the family, teachers, and other stakeholders involved in the child's care. Moreover, when we allow ourselves to be both creative and focused, we possess the power to impact entire communities.

Consider the following scenario: You have been working with a family for six months, regularly visiting their home. You have established a comfortable rapport with them, feeling at ease as you move around freely, even making yourself at home on the couch. Unfortunately, when the behavior technician resigns, leaving the client without immediate support, you offer to continue with Parent Collaboration across home and community settings until a replacement is found. However, the parent declines your offer. This rejection can be disheartening, but it often stems from the fact that the care you have been providing fails to address the family's primary concerns. If it does not feel personal to you, it will not feel personal to the family either. Consequently, the relationships we build with families can fall into two categories: they depend on us excessively, lack independence, or are indifferent because we have failed to make a meaningful impact.

So what's the sweet spot? BE DIFFERENT. A global survey by Gallup in 2020 found that approximately 20% of employees worldwide are actively engaged in their jobs. These individuals possess a strong connection to their work, are highly motivated, and actively contribute to their organization's success. The remaining 80% lack focus. To find the sweet spot, it is essential to pinpoint the problems during the assessment phase, align program goals with the family's priorities, and then ensure that your actions are in harmony with your values. Continuously revisiting those priorities will help ensure that you and your team keep your focus on what is truly important to the consumer. By doing so, you validate the parents' concerns and serve as a role model for intentional work. Witnessing your dedication and witnessing the subsequent positive outcomes will reinforce the practice of staying focused for everyone involved.

Value 4 - Precision

The importance of using data to make informed decisions cannot be overstated in any industry, particularly the service industry. Data-driven decision-making empowers businesses to make accurate predictions, identify trends, and optimize their strategies for success. When it comes to delivering services, getting it right the first time whenever possible becomes crucial, as it saves time and energy while strengthening consumer trust and belief in the science behind service delivery.

In the service industry, data provides valuable insights into customer preferences, needs, and behavior. By leveraging this information, businesses can customize their services to meet specific demands, resulting in higher customer satisfaction and loyalty. For instance, a hotel chain can use data on guest preferences, such as room amenities, preferred check-in times, or dietary restrictions, to provide personalized experiences. By getting these details right from the beginning, the hotel saves time and effort in rectifying any mistakes or complaints while building a positive reputation among its clientele.

The same is true for every industry that exists. In ABA, data-based decision-making starts right from the beginning, as we use data to make service recommendations, then use different types of data to steer our client programs. At the organizational level, data-driven decision-making helps us to optimize operational processes and maximize client outcomes. For example, a scheduling department can utilize client and staff availability and location data to plan and optimize employee schedules and driving routes. By analyzing historical data, they can identify peak hours, parent preferences, and other relevant factors, allowing them to allocate resources effectively and minimize staffing delays. This optimization not only saves time and energy for both the service provider and the consumers but also enhances the overall experience and reliability of the service.

Another critical aspect where data plays a vital role in the service industry is ensuring quality control and preventing errors. Businesses can identify patterns or indicators that may lead to service failures or customer dissatisfaction by collecting and analyzing data. For instance, a call center can monitor call metrics, such as average call duration, customer complaints, or agent performance, to identify areas for improvement. By addressing these issues proactively, they can reduce customer frustration, save time spent on resolving complaints, and enhance the quality of their service.

Furthermore, utilizing data in decision-making processes strengthens consumer trust and belief in the scientific approach behind service delivery. In today's data-driven world, consumers expect service providers to leverage available information to deliver efficient and effective services. When companies consistently make data-based decisions, consumers perceive them as more reliable, trustworthy, and professional. This, in turn, strengthens their confidence in the service provider and fosters long-term relationships, which are directly related to client outcomes.

Personal and Professional Policies

To avoid burnout, we must intentionally conduct our work in a way that fulfills us. We stay in our practice, focused on the key indicators to our own success and that of our clients, by implementing professional policies that correspond with and honor our personal values. Those values should be apparent in the policies with which we lead ourselves and others.

For example, a person who values time may ensure meeting efficiency by preparing an agenda beforehand and by refusing to veer off topic unless it is fundamentally necessary for driving the intended outcome of the meeting. Likewise, a person who values family may dive deep into building programs that address the values of the families they serve while maintaining a personal policy that forbids them from addressing client concerns on weekends. A leader who values their own autonomy and creativity may build their management style around training staff members to proficiency, empowering them to work independently, thus freeing up time to celebrate their employees' accomplishments. All of these are choices that we have the power to make daily. When we choose to consistently operate within our personal values, we meet our own intrinsic needs and make space for our highest contribution. Compassion fatigue is minimized, and *everybody benefits.*

Personal and professional policies can and should change as humans, leaders, or business owners evolve. The key is that we are intentional about using what we value to better understand how we can make a difference in the lives of others. By doing this, leaders model professional boundaries and their impact on our ability to consistently engage in effective clinical practices that yield better client outcomes and healthier workplace culture. In addition, conducting our work in a way that honors and acknowledges our own values and the values of others places the emphasis back on the client without neglecting the needs of the people serving them.

Chapter 3:
Radical Vision

I have been asked one recurring question throughout my career: "How do you meet your goals?" My reply is always, "I write them down." Listen, I don't do vision boards. In the words of my very sophisticated 4-year-old, "I'm not a fan."

Vision boards never sat right with me because no picture in a magazine is magnificent enough to hold my vision. When I envision my future, it's not things I see - *it's levels.* I find reducing my aspirations to photographs and poster boards limiting because it diminishes their significance. Vision boards are mere commonplace representations of something that can't be quantified. I see businesses (plural), communities, *and legacy.* Sometimes, it's just light. For a good portion of my workday, my head is literally in the clouds.

When I was a child, my great-grandmother reminded me of this verse: "Write the vision and make it plain on tablets so that a herald may run with it" (Habakkuk 2:2). I didn't understand it at the time. She passed one month after my 20th birthday and 2 years before I completed my undergraduate degree - I had *no idea* who I would become. But I'm convinced now that she did.

I spend a great deal of time one-on-one with my business. It's not uncommon for me to scribble an idea into a notebook, shove it into my desk drawer, and forget about it. In fact, it's very on-brand. I do it because, aside from being frazzled at times with my ideations, I know that everything I can imagine for my life and legacy will re-present itself at the right time. And when I think about the verse in its entirety, I think of all of the things that it takes to chase after a vision that no one else can see:

→ Clarity of Purpose

→ Communication and Execution

→ Patience and Persistence

→ Trust and Faith

Aligning an organization's identity with a personal vision requires courage and an unrelenting belief in something bigger than most can imagine, bigger than your ego, and for most of us, bigger than our bank accounts. Furthermore, persuading others to embrace that vision and execute it consistently, even when it goes against their own inclinations, often results in conflict. Conflict can be beneficial as long as it doesn't divert us from our goals. This is why before the end of this chapter, we will also discuss the importance of focus and how quickly we lose it when we feel as though our backs are up against the wall.

A Radical Vision

A company vision encapsulates a business's long-term goals, aspirations, and purpose. It is a forward-looking statement that outlines what the company aims to achieve and the impact it seeks to create in the world. A well-crafted vision provides a clear direction and acts as a guiding star for entrepreneurs and their teams. It is a source of inspiration, motivating individuals to work towards a shared purpose and align their efforts towards a common goal. A compelling vision also attracts stakeholders, including customers, employees, investors, and partners, who resonate with the company's mission and are more likely to engage with and support its endeavors. With a well-defined vision, entrepreneurs can foster a sense of purpose, drive innovation, and build a strong brand identity, ultimately increasing their chances of long-term success in a competitive marketplace.

In quarter 2 of 2023, I attended a business conference. During lunchtime, an older white gentleman walked over to the table a friend, and I were sitting at and asked us to save a spot for him. When he returned, he immediately kicked up a conversation by asking my friend and I where we were from. He seemed surprised to hear that we lived and worked less than 50 miles from LA, had driven in for the conference, and didn't work for the same company - we had each founded our own. He and his wife owned an ABA company in Hawaii that had been open for over 20 years. Between bites, he asked me about my vision and plans for my company's future. I told him I wanted to make quality ABA services more easily accessible in underrepresented communities by helping other black clinician-owned companies thrive.

The man straight-up said, "I don't think there's a market for that."
A market for what? I thought. *Quality healthcare for black people?*

I couldn't help but think that what he meant was that there was no way that a company that centers BIPOC individuals would yield the same ROI as a company that centers white families. He then went on to say that he was sure that I was the only person with that idea, so if I was going to go for it, I needed to move quickly. I was taken aback by his casual dismissal of what I had regarded as my life's work. But as he went back to shoveling his lunch into his mouth, I told him about Behavior Genius® and its 192% growth rate from 2020 to 2023 - from early COVID-19 to mid-recession. He stopped chewing, raised a brow as if to indicate and hide his amusement, then shrugged. When he got up from the table, he told me that he was from Washington, DC, where approximately 50% of the population identified as Black. And that I should call him if I was ever interested in partnering.

I smiled to myself all the way back to my seat. A year earlier, I sat in that same seat, feeling like I didn't belong. And on this day, I had unapologetically defended my *(black-ass)* vision because it was clear to ME. I found it interesting that we had both attended the conference as the outcome of or in pursuit of, our visions for our organizations. My vision was one for people; his was one for money. *Both visions had the power to influence our industry.*

A Radical Mission

While a vision is a desired future state or aspiration, a mission is a statement of purpose and the actions taken to achieve that vision. To find your mission, it is essential to reflect on your passions, values, and the impact you wish to make. Consider what problems you want to solve, the values you want your company to embody, and the legacy you want to leave behind. Conducting market research, seeking feedback from potential customers, and assessing their societal and environmental needs can also help you shape a mission that resonates with your target audience and fulfills a meaningful purpose.

Your mission shapes your message, and your message is your word.

Brand integrity is essential to the dissemination of your company's mission. I have learned that business owners cannot be solely responsible for spreading the word and ensuring it resonates with people. We need a team of "heralds," especially if we are scaling. Most of us don't get paid for using social media to share the details of our last Target run. We market the brand freely, and not because we share their values because, let's be honest, you were today years old when you learned that Target's core values are inclusivity, connection, and drive. We share simply because our shopping trip was pleasant or we overspent again, which only speaks to how little self-control we have or how much we love Target. At the end of every day, unconditionally for most of us, we are diehard Bullseye champions. Whoever is responsible for developing this company's vision has both our attention and our utmost respect.

Recognizing who your champions are is good for morale and can significantly impact the success and growth of a company. Your champions are individuals who passionately believe in the organization's mission and values and actively work towards disseminating and representing this vision to others. By identifying and rewarding these employees, organizations can foster a culture of dedication, drive, and engagement that encourages connection and propels the organization toward its goals.

Champions are influencers that act as ambassadors for the company's mission. When employees genuinely believe in their work, they naturally become enthusiastic advocates for the organization. They communicate the company's values to colleagues, clients, and the wider community, effectively spreading the message and helping to build a positive brand reputation.

Moreover, champions can also serve as a valuable source of feedback and ideas for the organization. Their deep understanding of the mission and front-line experience equips them with unique insights into what works and what needs improvement. By regularly engaging with these employees and seeking their input, organizations can tap into a wealth of knowledge and leverage it to drive innovation, refine strategies, and enhance overall performance.

Expressing gratitude toward the champions within an organization is of paramount importance. These individuals embody the mission and values of the company and act as powerful catalysts for growth and success. By acknowledging their positive behaviors, organizations not only encourage their ongoing dedication but also inspire others to join in the pursuit of the shared vision. Through their passion, advocacy, and influence, champions drive positive change and progress, ultimately propelling the organization toward its desired outcomes.

Radical Focus

Toni Morrison, one of the most celebrated black female authors of my mother's time and mine, wrote, "The function, the very serious function of racism is a distraction. It keeps you from doing your work. It keeps you explaining, over and over again, your reason for being." Given the fact that racism has resulted in hundreds of direct and indirect outcomes, trauma responses, and intergenerational patterns, I believe this statement to be encompassing of all of the effects of racism as well. As people of color, we are more likely to procrastinate before completing a job application because we inherently feel underqualified; we walk into every interview with trepidation and feelings of inadequacy, and we walk out feeling a sense of uncertainty and judgment - and then we do the work of trying to figure out whether or not we are just being hypersensitive and whether or not our reticence showed. We get the job and engage in self-talk all the way to the office about what we need to bring to the table and how we're going to kill it on *day one*. And then comes the invisible workload - the onslaught of *isms* - self-criticism, perfectionism, sensationalism by our peers, and cynicism from our managers.

Some of us spend more time trying to prove and disprove than we do being engaged in our work in a way that fulfills *us*. We have been conditioned to operate under radical pressure. And when we are under pressure, we lose sight of our priorities - to protect the mission, to share the vision, and to focus only on what drives the intended outcome. A leader without focus develops a team that lacks focus. I have experienced firsthand what happens when a team loses focus. And I'm not referring to having an unmotivated team. I'm talking about when the team loses sight of what is of immediate importance from day to day. When even the strongest team members are focused on jumping through hoops that are not mission-critical.

Not to mention, we are distracted as a nation. Current events and social media have only highlighted this fact. In the United States, distractions have become an inherent part of the national landscape, diverting attention from pressing issues and societal challenges. One prevalent form of distraction is the constant barrage of media consumption, with people spending hours scrolling through social media feeds, streaming endless entertainment content, and becoming engrossed in the latest viral trends. The proliferation of smartphones and gadgets has further amplified this distraction culture, pulling individuals away from real-world interactions and diverting their focus to virtual realms.

Additionally, the fast-paced nature of American life, characterized by long work hours and a culture of multitasking, leaves little room for reflection or introspection. The 24-hour news cycle and sensationalized media coverage also divert attention from critical matters, as news outlets often prioritize sensationalism over in-depth analysis. Furthermore, the increasing polarization of society has led to a constant state of distraction, as individuals are consumed by divisive political debates, ideological conflicts, and the amplification of echo chambers. This is even true in Behavior Analysis, where opposing opinions about the science and the demonstration of it have served only to divide clinicians at all levels and breed doubt in the eyes of the families we serve.

It has become increasingly more challenging to engage in meaningful dialogue, address complex issues, and collectively work towards solutions, thus perpetuating the cycle of distraction in the workplace. This is the world that our businesses operate in. It is the world that our employees go home to. But it doesn't have to be how we build up our operations. Sometimes, we get so busy *being busy* that we are completely oblivious to the fact that we are not productive. And at our worst, we are *counterproductive.* As leaders, we must take up the courage to move in a way that radically protects our vision. We are accountable for ensuring that every team member recognizes that not everything is essential or aligned with the organization's mission. And that things that are important are not always urgent. And that things that are urgent are not always *our* emergencies.

Radical Demand

I vividly remember the day I realized I was stuck in a hamster wheel, focused only on running. I wasn't pausing often enough to rest, recharge, or reflect on everything I had done right in my business. I set targets, solicited feedback, made corrections on the fly, and kept it pushin'. But that week had been a week of enlightenment for me. I had spent the weekend in Detroit, Michigan, at the Black Behavior Analyst Conference. It was the first time in my career that I had shown up with all of those "first day" jitters, and I wasn't met with a push to prove myself. That weekend, everyone around me was honest about how exhausted we were and why. That Friday, I went to lunch with my family. We spent what felt like hours researching the best black-owned restaurants in Detroit. It was Juneteenth weekend, and we had all agreed that we would be damned if we traveled all that way not to be on our *black shit.* So, we followed a friend's recommendation to visit Trap Vegan.

When we walked into the restaurant, I immediately started making observations - *The line is out the door, and it is filled with all kinds of people - young, old, black, white, couples, and families. That must mean the food is good.* We waited about 15 minutes before we placed our order. As we waited, I watched how the staff worked quickly in the back, calling out information about each order and double-checking to ensure each order was correct before calling out the next number. Inside seating was limited, and there was no seating outside, so people came and went. As we approached the front of the line, I noticed that the cashier taking orders was also directing the rest of the team, yet she remained calm the entire time and looked every single customer in the eye when they spoke. I started to assume that she was the manager or the owner. The lady in front of me complained about how disappointed she was with the wait. She had already paid for her food; However, she went back and forth with the cashier despite the long line behind her. The manager (I'm convinced now that she was at least the leader of the pack) listened attentively to the woman's concerns for a few minutes before issuing her a refund, and I will never forget what she said to her: "I'm sorry ma'am, but we are understaffed. And because we are understaffed and have a whole line here waiting, we just don't have the time for difficult customers. I have issued you a refund with a little extra change. Thank you so much for understanding." She smiled and nodded at the woman, waiting for her to leave the counter. The woman took her money, said that she understood, and left.

When I reached the counter, the manager smiled as though nothing had happened, greeted me, and asked to take my order. A sign on the glass to her right read, *"The entire world is understaffed. Please be kind to the ones who showed up."* I snapped a photo, placed my order, and waited patiently as I watched this woman and her team keep doing what they were there to do - serve the people. They did not stop to entertain anything that interrupted their flow. Every person who waited in line that day ate and left happy and full.

I learned a valuable lesson that day. There is so much work to be done in our field. ABA business owners have allowed the increasing demand to dictate the pace, quality, and framework of our services. In his book, "The One Thing," Gary Keller kicked off his introduction with a Russian Proverb: "If you chase two rabbits, you will not catch either one." The book challenges the reader to focus on the one thing that will produce the *most* outstanding results and chase that. In ABA (and I would argue that this is true in the healthcare sector), service delivery is the "one thing." Now, if you think that "quality" would be the one thing, consider the fact that for quality practices to occur, the service must be delivered consistently in the first place. Suppose we assume that all Behavior Analysts possess equal capabilities. In that case, the one who always shows up seizes multiple chances to build rapport with the family, guides the behavior technician, and conducts valuable observations to continuously enhance the program would likely experience increased rates of retaining front-line staff, greater adherence to treatment protocols, and improved outcomes for the family. If service delivery was the main focus, organizations would shift ethically and financially.

Instead, some of us sit in our board meetings with the best intentions and set marketing goals while our waitlists continue to climb. Employee turnover is out of control, and parents complain about inconsistent service delivery. Our talent acquisition team is pressured to build larger cohorts by hiring underqualified staff. The training department cannot provide an intimate and optimal environment for new, inexperienced staff to learn, so clinical supervisors are expected to pick up the slack and train on the job. I favor on-the-job training. But the Behavior Analysts of today have plates full of distractions. So, they check in physically (when they can and contingent on the size of their caseloads) and check out mentally. The Behavior Tech resigns, the child regresses, the parents complain, the organization pushes to fill the seat, and the cycle continues.

And the families are hurting.

And our teams are burnt out.

And CEOs are exhausted.

And our field is at risk.

All for lack of a collective focus.

And you didn't ask for it, but here's the tea: Half of the employees who resign leave the field and assume that it's just not for them, making service delivery increasingly impossible. The other half jump from agency to agency, hoping for something better but realizing that we are all unfocused and reacting to the same contingencies, regardless of our vision, mission, or values. What would happen if we all stopped reacting to the madness and started responding with intention toward our *united vision* - and nothing else?

That week after Detroit, having a radical vision meant acknowledging the ways in which I had perpetuated the engagement in work that did not push forward my vision. It meant choosing to protect my team following an investigation into a parent's concern by resisting the urge to call and offer the family an immediate solution to an unreasonable request.

It meant coming to terms with the fact that the company I had built was not what I had envisioned. My vision was never to grow my company at a rapid rate. It wasn't to make millions of dollars, it wasn't to people please, and it certainly wasn't to join the assembly line of fast-food-style service delivery models that have invaded the ABA space.

There is a standard of quality in our industry that minimizes the impact of cultural awareness, humility, and competence on Behavioral outcomes for children with special needs. My intention is to raise the bar on that standard. As such, my team and I are committed to a collective demonstration of diversity, equity, and inclusion that centers on thrivable workspaces, inclusive service delivery models, and meaningful connections to the people in the communities that we serve.

Anything that distracts us from carrying out that specific vision will no longer be reinforced by any member of my team. *That's the strategy.*

Chapter 4:
Radical Strategy

As the HBIC of a rapidly evolving venture, I have realized that while quick growth can be exhilarating, it also presents unique challenges that strain an organization's operations. There is undoubtedly a daily struggle that comes along with scaling a company, and no company is exempt. Without a clear documented framework or strategy, our success largely rested on my strategic mindset and decision-making abilities. However, to sustain our growth and build a resilient organization, I realized that we needed more than just executors to continue to be successful as a corporation. The organization's fate could not continue to rest solely on a single individual's vision. We needed more visionaries at the leadership level, and when the rubber started to meet the road, we had two options: We could search for them or keep our team intact and build them up.

In this chapter, we will delve into the profound impact of strategic thinking and how it can transform the dynamics within an organization. By engaging in strategic conversations and leveraging the principles of Organizational Behavior Management (OBM), we can empower our teams to think and act strategically.

Strategy is the lifeblood of any successful organization. It provides a roadmap, a North Star that guides every decision, action, and resource allocation. Without a well-defined strategy, even the most talented and motivated teams can find themselves lost in a sea of possibilities, their efforts scattered and uncoordinated. As I have experienced firsthand, and maybe you have too, relying solely on individual strategic thinking can lead to inconsistent outcomes and a lack of cohesive direction. We need a radical shift in our approach.

To foster a culture of collaborative thinking and action, executive leaders should employ the principles of OBM to effectively convey their strategic objectives. By doing so, we can ensure that the actions and behaviors of individual employees reflect the organization's values and align with its strategic direction. By promoting team alignment, long-term success can be achieved.

Planning For Success: A Four-Step Cycle For Leaders

The idea of planning often gets more attention than any of the other critical steps to accomplishing a goal. But let's be honest: If writing

SMART goals were the only way to reach the finish line, we'd all be lapping our competition. While millions of people make New Year's resolutions as a re-up on their goals, few hit their target before the end of the year.

This raises a few questions: Are we as effective at execution as we are at planning? Furthermore, are we as effective at planning as we think we are? Organizations do not fail for lack of good ideas; they fail due to ineffective planning and poor execution. Goals that accelerate the growth of an organization require a commitment to the process. To move the needle and achieve greater success, leaders must learn to follow a specific process wherein they master the art of thinking, planning, executing, and pivoting — in that order.

STEP 1: Think

In the book "Essentialism" by Greg McKeown, the concept of "WIN" (What's Important Now?) plays a crucial role in achieving organizational success through focused decision-making and efficient resource allocation. McKeown highlights the significance of adopting a disciplined approach to identify and pursue the most essential priorities within an organization. The "WIN" concept guides leaders to align their efforts and resources with what truly matters, ensuring optimal performance and sustainable growth.

At every stage, executive leaders need help prioritizing their work and making solid decisions because they spend most of their time thinking about unimportant things. We know that running a business requires brainpower, but most entrepreneurs and executives have yet to learn what they should be thinking *about*. This is because we are required to change our thought patterns depending on the role we are playing within an organization.

As an executive, you must master the art of thinking in systems. Much like a machine, an organization is composed of multiple parts. Each part of the system serves a function that contributes to the whole. To understand how to plan for success, what to measure, and when to switch gears, you must recognize the total system as the sum of its parts. From there, you must understand how each piece is connected to and impacts the others.

Entrepreneurs are overwhelmed with numerous tasks, responsibilities, and challenges in today's fast-paced and ever-evolving business landscape. The ability to effectively narrow their focus and identify what truly matters amidst the chaos is crucial for success. Executive leaders should follow a practical framework that will enable them and their teams to prioritize their thoughts and align them with the most critical objectives. By considering the desired outcome, evaluating possible effects, and selecting appropriate measurements, leaders can enhance their decision-making process and achieve meaningful results.

Define the Desired Outcome

Before delving into daily tasks and obligations, it is vital for leaders to clearly define the desired outcome. This involves envisioning the end goal and understanding what needs to be accomplished. A clear vision of the desired outcome can anchor our thoughts and actions. This process helps filter out distractions and ensure that efforts are directed toward what truly matters. Leaders can ask themselves questions such as:

1. What am I trying to achieve in the short term and long term?

2. What specific results or objectives do I want to accomplish?

3. How does this align with my broader business goals and purpose?

Consider Possible Outcomes

Once the desired outcome has been established, leaders need to explore various potential outcomes that may arise during the journey. This step involves analyzing different scenarios and evaluating their implications. We can anticipate challenges, risks, and opportunities by considering possible outcomes, allowing us to develop a more robust and adaptive mindset. This process also helps leaders to identify the most efficient path forward, as we can weigh the pros and cons of each potential outcome. To facilitate this analysis, leaders can follow these steps:

1. Brainstorm various possible outcomes that could result from pursuing the desired effect.

2. Evaluate the feasibility, benefits, and drawbacks of each potential outcome.

3. Consider the resources, constraints, and external factors that may influence the likelihood of each outcome.

Select Appropriate Measurements

Ahhh - My favorite part! We need to establish reasonable and relevant measurements to assess progress and determine when the desired outcome has been achieved. Measures serve as benchmarks that enable leaders to track progress, make informed adjustments, and celebrate milestones. When selecting measurements, leaders should consider the following:

1. *Quantifiable Metrics:* Identify specific, measurable metrics that can be used to evaluate progress toward the desired outcome. These metrics may include sales figures, customer satisfaction ratings, or productivity indicators.

2. *Key Performance Indicators (KPIs):* Determine the key indicators directly contributing to the desired outcome. These KPIs act as early warning signals and provide insight into the effectiveness of strategies and initiatives.

3. *Timeframes:* Define a timeline within which the desired outcome should be achieved. This allows leaders to establish deadlines and

create a sense of urgency, facilitating focused and timely action for ourselves and our teams.

4. *Adjustability:* Remain open to adjusting the measurements as the circumstances evolve. Regularly reassess the relevance and effectiveness of the chosen measures and make necessary adaptations to ensure they remain aligned with the desired outcome.

By following a systematic approach to focusing our thoughts, executive leaders and entrepreneurs can navigate the complexities of their roles more effectively. By clarifying the desired outcome, considering potential outcomes, and selecting appropriate measurements, we can prioritize our efforts and channel our energy toward what truly matters. This disciplined approach enables leaders to make well-informed data-based decisions, adapt to changing circumstances, and ultimately achieve our business objectives with greater clarity and confidence.

STEP 2: Plan

To achieve success in any entrepreneurial endeavor, it is crucial to have a clear and executable plan in place. Leaders should choose a planning style and frequency that reflects the time and resources they have to complete the goal. For instance, you may have one annual goal that you can break down into quarterly or monthly benchmarks.

While it may be tempting to give ourselves permission to redraft our plans as we go, building the plane while you are flying can result in a lack of direction and clarity. With a well-thought-out plan, the organization can define its objectives, identify the necessary steps to achieve them, and communicate a clear vision to employees. This ambiguity can lead to confusion, inefficiency, and a lack of alignment among team members. In addition, when you build the plane while flying, you are forced to make decisions on the spot without sufficient time for analysis and reflection. This reactive decision-making can be hasty, based on incomplete information, and prone to errors. It increases the risk of making poor choices that may have long-term consequences for the organization.

With a solid plan, it becomes easier to allocate resources effectively. You may find yourself constantly adjusting priorities, reallocating resources on the fly, and struggling to meet deadlines. This lack of resource planning can lead to inefficiencies, wasted resources, and increased costs. It also often leads to increased stress and burnout. Poor planning can create a high-stress environment for the executive leader and the entire organization. Constantly reacting and making decisions without a clear plan can be overwhelming. The lack of structure and certainty can also demotivate employees and affect their productivity and engagement.

Planning is crucial for setting long-term goals and mapping the path to achieving them. When you set out without a strategic plan, the focus is primarily on short-term fixes and immediate challenges. This approach can hinder you and your team's ability to think strategically and limit your capacity to shape the organization's future.

Begin with the End in Mind

To set a clear and executable plan, it is essential to determine what the "end" will look like for both you and your organization. This involves envisioning your ultimate goals and objectives and then working backward to identify the necessary steps. By starting with a clear vision of the end result, you can align your planning efforts toward achieving that outcome.

Choose a Planning Style and Frequency

Selecting a planning style and frequency that suits your organization's needs and available resources is important. Consider the time and resources required to accomplish your goals effectively. For example, you may have an annual goal that can be broken down into quarterly or monthly benchmarks. Choosing a planning style that aligns with your resources ensures that your plan remains actionable and manageable for the entire team.

Write Time-Based Goals with Specific Deadlines

Setting time-based goals with specific deadlines is a fundamental aspect of effective planning. It is easiest to conduct planning quarterly.

Allocate a few hours at the end of each quarter to prepare for the following quarter. During this time, review your progress, assess what needs to be continued, eliminated, or added to your plan, and establish new milestones. Quarterly planning allows you to track progress, gather necessary data, and break down long-term goals into manageable steps.

Make Predictions and Identify Potential Obstacles

While planning, it is also essential to gauge the best path forward by making predictions wherever possible. Consider potential challenges and obstacles that may arise along the way. You can better prepare for potential setbacks and develop contingency plans by being specific in your predictions. Additionally, involving other critical thinkers on your team can provide valuable insights and help identify gaps in your plan. Avoid leaping into action before thoroughly examining and understanding the potential risks and challenges.

Make it Plain

Clarity is the key to successful organizational planning. The clearer and more concise your plan is, the easier it will be to execute. Clearly define your goals, strategies, and action steps. Avoid ambiguity and ensure that all team members understand their roles and responsibilities. Clarity allows for a shared understanding and alignment within the organization, promoting effective execution.

Document and reference your plan

Once you have developed a clear plan, documentation is key. Whether you write it down in a notebook, use a digital project management app, or create sticky notes, it is crucial to get your thoughts out on paper. Documenting your plan provides a tangible reference that can be revisited and updated as needed. Regularly refer to your plan to stay focused, track progress, and make adjustments when necessary. A well-crafted plan serves as a roadmap to success and ensures that efforts are aligned, resources are optimized, and progress is tracked.

STEP 3: Execute

There needs to be more than a well-crafted plan to achieve success. To ensure the effective execution of your strategic plan, you must actively engage and leverage your team. Nailing your plan involves identifying key stakeholders, establishing buy-in, delegating responsibilities, developing a strategic communication strategy, and managing the process continuously.

Engaging Key Stakeholders

Once your planning is complete, it's time to involve your key stakeholders in the execution process. Key stakeholders may include department heads, managers, and team members who will be directly impacted by the strategic plan. By involving them early on, you establish buy-in and foster a sense of ownership among your team members. Clearly communicate what the process will look like for the organization and how it will affect their roles. Encourage questions and address any concerns they may have, ensuring they understand the plan's benefits and rationale.

Be careful not to overshare information. While dropping hints to various team members may seem innocent, some people panic at just the thought of an impending change. The last thing you want is to leave room for speculation about the plan before it is fully implemented. Decide early on who is on the need-to-know list and ensure that your leadership team is aware of confidentiality so that all communication regarding the plan remains consistent throughout implementation.

Delegating Responsibilities

Successful execution requires delegation. Clearly define the responsibilities of each team member and align them with the strategic objectives. Assigning specific tasks and roles ensures accountability and empowers individuals to contribute actively to the plan's execution. Moreover, consider the interdependencies between team members and stakeholders. Identify potential collaborations and promote teamwork to foster a sense of collective responsibility.

Strategic Communication

To achieve successful execution, transparent communication is paramount. Share every new initiative's what, who, when, and why whenever possible. Clearly articulate the goals, objectives, and desired outcomes of the strategic plan. Ensure that your team understands their role in the process and the roles of other stakeholders they may need to collaborate with. This clarity and transparency minimize confusion and increase overall alignment.

Different people absorb information in different ways. Therefore, to maximize understanding and engagement, diversify your communication channels. Utilize written, visual, and verbal formats to convey information effectively. Written communication, such as emails, memos, or project updates, provides a formal record of information. Visual aids, such as charts, diagrams, or presentations, help illustrate complex concepts. Verbal communication, through team meetings or one-on-one conversations, allows for immediate clarification and discussion. By diversifying communication channels, you accommodate varying communication preferences and increase the likelihood of understanding for all team members.

Continuous Management

Executing a strategic plan is an ongoing process that requires continuous management. Monitor progress regularly, track milestones, and celebrate achievements. Establish measurable markers throughout the execution timeline to evaluate progress objectively. Frequent check-ins with your team provide an opportunity to address challenges, provide support, and realign efforts, if necessary. By consistently managing the execution process, you demonstrate your commitment to the plan's success and maintain momentum within your team.

Effective execution of a strategic plan relies on your team's active involvement and engagement. Change can be met with resistance, so creating an environment where individuals feel informed, supported, and empowered is essential. Through effective leadership and leveraging your team's collective talents and efforts, you can ensure the clean execution of your strategic plan and achieve the desired organizational outcomes.

STEP 4: Pivot

If there is one thing that we all know when it comes to business, it's that change is inevitable. No matter how meticulously you plan your strategic initiatives, unexpected circumstances that require you to shift direction can arise. The ability to pivot effectively is essential for executive leaders who seek to navigate through uncertainty and ensure the success of their organizations.

Whether you plan to pivot or not, the reality is that you will likely face situations that necessitate a change in direction. Embracing the concept of pivoting from the outset of your strategic planning helps to reduce frustration and promotes a proactive mindset. By acknowledging that change is a natural part of the process, you position yourself as a leader who is ready to respond to unexpected challenges rather than being caught off guard. While others may resort to panic when faced with a need to pivot, you will be prepared and equipped to make informed decisions.

At its core, to "pivot" means to change direction based on the circumstances at hand. However, successful pivoting requires a deep understanding of your organization's goals, market dynamics, and available resources. It is not a haphazard reaction but a calculated adjustment that aligns with your strategic objectives. A well-executed pivot can open up new opportunities and help you overcome obstacles that may have hindered progress toward your goals.

Determining when to pivot is a critical aspect of strategic planning. Data analysis is crucial in identifying areas of circular causality or potential bottlenecks in your plan. Monitoring key performance indicators (KPIs) and relevant market trends will provide valuable insights into the effectiveness of your current strategies. It is essential to gather enough data to justify a change without allowing a potential issue to persist for too long, as this could lead to detrimental consequences.

Even with the most precise planning, continuous evaluation of progress is necessary. Regular check-ins at 30, 60, and 90-day intervals can help you assess the effectiveness of your strategies, identify areas that require adjustment, and monitor the development of desired outcomes. This iterative approach allows you to implement changes, address any operational challenges, and observe the impact of your adjustments. By embracing this process, you create a culture of adaptability within your organization and foster a mindset that values ongoing improvement.

Just like any skill, the ability to pivot effectively improves with practice. The more you expose yourself and your team to various situations, the better you become at predicting outcomes and making informed decisions. This is why it is important to encourage a learning mindset and provide opportunities for team members to tackle challenges and embrace change. Through practice and experience, you develop a sense of intuition and confidence in navigating through uncertainty successfully.

Strategic plans are not set in stone but rather adaptable frameworks that require continuous evaluation and adjustment. By mastering the art of strategic planning and all of its steps, you will empower yourself and your team to run the play efficiently and effectively, setting up your organization to thrive in an evolving world.

Chapter 5:
Radical Systems

Throughout history, minority-owned businesses have played a vital role in shaping economies and communities. Despite numerous challenges, these enterprises have displayed resilience and become crucial contributors to economic growth and diversity. This article explores the history of minority-owned businesses, their success rates, and the impact of poor processes on business development and long-term success.

Minority-owned businesses have a rich history rooted in overcoming adversities and systemic barriers. In the United States, African American entrepreneurs faced significant challenges during the era of slavery and segregation. The end of legal segregation in the 1960s and the subsequent Civil Rights Movement paved the way for greater opportunities for minority business owners. Similarly, Hispanic, Asian, Native American, and other minority communities also faced various hurdles but have made significant strides in establishing successful businesses.

Success Rates of Minority-Owned Businesses

While it is important to acknowledge the achievements of minority-owned businesses, it is equally crucial to recognize the persistent disparities that exist. Success rates vary among different minority groups due to various factors, including access to capital, systemic biases, and limited networking opportunities.

Limited Access to Capital:

Access to capital remains a significant challenge for minority-owned businesses. Studies indicate that minority entrepreneurs often face higher barriers when seeking loans or investment capital than their white counterparts. Limited access to financial resources can hinder growth opportunities, making it difficult for minority-owned businesses to scale and compete effectively.

When I founded Behavior Genius, I didn't even know what capital was. I mean, of course, I had heard the word before, and certainly, I knew that it had something to do with the money that wealthy people used to make investments and pay operating expenses in their businesses. But I had so many questions when it came to capital:

→ What types of capital are there?

→ When should I be applying for capital?

→ What will it cost me to pay it all back?

So the last thing I needed to worry about was whether I would ever be approved.

Systemic Biases and Discrimination:

Historically, minority-owned businesses have faced discriminatory practices and systemic biases that affect our success rates. These biases can manifest in various forms, such as lower credit ratings, biased lending practices, and limited access to lucrative markets. Discrimination and prejudice can hinder business growth and impede minority entrepreneurs from fully realizing their potential.

In the field of Behavior Analysis, this reality releases pressure that extends beyond the business owner and straight out to the client. When minority-owned business owners are denied equal access to the tools they need to thrive, there is a trickle-down effect - Minority children in underrepresented communities are also less likely to receive access to quality behavioral healthcare. One reason for this is that where there is limited minority representation in an organization or industry, there is also limited diversity of thought. In these cases, innovation is based on capitalist gains, and there is little to no regard for the population's needs.

I once attended a presentation on expanding Autism services across multiple markets (or to new states). The speaker was asked how an ABA provider should go about deciding where to grow their business next. The response: "First and foremost, check the Medi-Cal rates in the area, and if they are not sustainable, don't expand there." After I picked my jaw up out of my lap, I realized something that I wish I could unlearn because the ethical and moral implications of it rattle me to this day: Thousands of our people are being intentionally excluded from receiving access to a service that they desperately need, and that is their birthright. *Ain't nobody is coming to save us.*

Limited Networking Opportunities:

Networking plays a crucial role in the success of any business. Unfortunately, minority-owned companies often have limited access to influential networks and connections that can open doors to new markets, partnerships, and funding opportunities. This lack of access can create barriers to growth and limit the chances of long-term success.

If you're anything like me, then you hate networking. This is why I was in the field for nearly two decades before I ever attended a business conference. And when I started attending them, I was immediately reminded why I had declined the opportunity all those years. I didn't feel like I belonged. On top of being a wallflower all my life, I knew that I would have to play politics and code-switch to be accepted at Behavior

Analysis conferences. I also knew there would be little to no representation among presenters, so I would take it personally if I was ignored or unseen. And who could blame me, considering the fact that statistically, I didn't stand a chance of making any connections?

But what I learned from attending and leaning in is that when we attend networking events, we unlock a world of opportunities for collaboration with other like-minded professionals. Granted, we may have to fish further to find the right tribe. Still, nonetheless, there are people who understand the importance of allyship in helping to remove systemic barriers and their influence on healthcare equity.

The Impact of Poor or Nonexistent Processes

Effective processes and operational strategies are crucial for any business's development and long-term success, regardless of ownership. However, minority-owned companies, like any other enterprise, can suffer if they lack proper processes. Here are some of the consequences of poor or nonexistent processes:

Operational Inefficiencies

Without well-defined processes, businesses may face inefficiencies, redundancies, and inconsistencies in their operations. This can lead to increased costs, delayed deliveries, and customer dissatisfaction. Such operational inefficiencies can erode profitability and hinder the overall success of minority-owned businesses.

Let's consider a scenario in the Applied Behavior Analysis (ABA) industry that we know all too well. In this example, operational inefficiency occurs in the scheduling department of an ABA agency.

During client intake, the scheduling department is responsible for assigning therapists to clients based on their availability, language, location, matching the therapist's skills to the child's specific needs, and ensuring that therapy sessions are scheduled in a timely manner. However, operational inefficiency arises due to a lack of proper coordination, effective communication, and clear, *task-analyzed workflows* within the scheduling department.

Here's a detailed example of how this inefficiency can lead to increased costs for the organization:

1. Missed or delayed therapy sessions: The scheduling department fails to correctly assign therapists to clients, leading to missed or delayed therapy sessions. For example, a child might be assigned a therapist who lives too far from the family's home, resulting in the cancellation or rescheduling of sessions. This inconsistency in therapy sessions can disrupt the child's progress and delay their development.

2. Increased staff turnover: When therapists' schedules are mismanaged or their preferences are not considered, it can lead to

frustration and dissatisfaction among the staff. This can increase staff turnover as therapists seek more reliable or flexible employment opportunities. High staff turnover rates can disrupt the continuity of care for children. New therapists need time to familiarize themselves with each child's unique needs and develop an effective therapeutic relationship.

3. Inefficient travel time and expenses: Poor scheduling practices can result in therapists traveling extensively between different locations throughout the day. This leads to inefficiencies in travel time and increased transportation costs. If therapists spend significant time commuting between sessions, it reduces the time spent providing therapy, ultimately reducing the overall productivity of the agency.

4. Administrative overhead: Inaccurate or inefficient scheduling may increase administrative overhead. For instance, rescheduling missed sessions, coordinating with therapists and families, and handling complaints or grievances require additional administrative effort and resources. This can lead to increased staffing needs in the scheduling department or additional administrative tasks for other staff members, contributing to higher costs.

5. Lower client satisfaction: When therapy sessions are missed, delayed, or inconsistent, it can result in lower client satisfaction.

Parents or caregivers may become frustrated with the agency's inability to provide consistent and reliable services. Dissatisfied families may choose to discontinue services, seek alternative providers, or voice their concerns, which can harm the agency's reputation and potentially lead to a loss of future clients.

These operational inefficiencies in the scheduling department can result in increased costs for the ABA agency due to missed therapy sessions, increased staff turnover, inefficient travel time and expenses, higher administrative overhead, and lower client satisfaction. It highlights the importance of effective scheduling practices to optimize resources, enhance client outcomes, and reduce unnecessary organizational costs.

I once had a manager ask me one question whenever I proposed a process change: *"Portia, have you considered whether this is a process problem or a people problem?"* The answer was always yes. Pinpointing the underlying problem is like OBM 101. But his asking of the question forced me to dig deeper if merely to prove my point. That's what great questions do. I learned that before proposing solutions, I needed to know what had caused the problem. *Was it my team's ineffective time management? Was the instruction unclear? Was turnover so frequent that, at times, virtually every employee was under-trained?*

Knowing the answers to these questions helped me ask for the right thing, which made my intervention more effective. Behavior Analysts are familiar with pinpointing when implementing client programs. This process mirrors the part of the Functional Behavioral Assessment (FBA) where we interview and observe, listing independent variables and assessing barriers and skill deficits that impact performance.

If I didn't have the data to prove that my team was leading with optimal performance, then I had no businesses requesting a laborious process change or a software purchase. Especially one that, if implemented prematurely, would increase tech and labor costs for the organization. It would also free my team of the honorable responsibility of doing their damn jobs and improving their individual and collective productivity.

Ineffective Financial Management

Proper financial processes and controls can result in better cash flow management, accurate financial reporting, and difficulties securing funding. Sound financial processes, including budgeting, forecasting, and tracking expenses, are essential for the sustainable growth of minority-owned businesses.

The last - and I mean the *very last* thing that any business owner wants is ineffective processes surrounding their finances. Can you imagine not having the tools to make financial decisions at your house? Now let's be real - not many of us actually run our personal finances on a strict budget or even have clear savings goals. But let's talk about something we are all familiar with: *Paying Bills.* Our credit reports are full of data that reveals the effectiveness of our personal financial systems. Personal financial processes may include setting up autopay, adherence to pay schedules, and using and paying credit cards.

People with poor systems or no systems around their finances tend to have more difficulty making on-time payments and maintaining a good credit history. For business owners, having processes that ensure that all invoices are received and that the bills are paid on time is critical to the organization's and its stakeholders' performance.

Missed Growth Opportunities

A lack of streamlined processes can hinder the ability of minority-owned businesses to identify and capitalize on growth opportunities. Poor processes may lead to slow decision-making, delayed service delivery and development, and inadequate market research. This can result in missed opportunities and lost competitive advantages.

For example, an ABA agency may need more efficient intake and assessment processes. If the agency needs a streamlined system for efficiently evaluating and onboarding new clients, it may experience delays in initiating therapy services. This can result in missed opportunities to serve a more extensive client base and expand their business. Additionally, a cumbersome intake process may deter potential clients from seeking services, further limiting the agency's growth potential.

Furthermore, the lack of streamlined billing and reimbursement processes can be another hindrance. Minority-owned ABA agencies may need help navigating complex insurance procedures and reimbursement systems. Delays or errors in billing and reimbursement can lead to financial strain and reduced cash flow, impeding the agency's ability to invest in growth initiatives, such as hiring additional therapists or expanding into new geographic areas.

Additionally, ineffective staff management processes, such as inadequate training or communication protocols, can hinder the agency's ability to provide high-quality services consistently, which can impact its reputation and limit its growth potential.

Addressing operational inefficiencies is critical for optimizing performance, promoting equitable growth, and enhancing the organization's impact.

Processes are a Gift that Keeps on Giving

Despite facing numerous challenges, minority-owned businesses have made significant contributions to the economic landscape. Limited access to capital, systemic biases, and a lack of networking opportunities remain substantial obstacles. Additionally, better processes are needed to ensure business development and long-term success. To foster the growth of minority-owned businesses, addressing these challenges by promoting equitable access to resources, combating systemic biases, and emphasizing the importance of effective systems is essential.

Streamlined processes are the gift that keeps on giving. Having them in place helps to alleviate communication breakdowns between departments, among team members, and between the organization and the client. Ultimately, better communication leads to more consistent execution, which enhances the overall experience for everyone.

To be clear, there is always a process at play - a way we carry out our work. The question is whether or not those systems are making or breaking us. Take procrastination, an age-old habit I have yet to break. The process is that we wait until the week before an assignment is due. Then, we survive that week by ordering takeout and Door-Dashing americanos from Starbucks every night. We stay up later than usual, blast 90's Hip-Hop and R&B, bang out the assignment, meet the deadline, and reward ourselves with a Frappuccino.

While this method worked for me across my entire academic and adult career, I understand that:

1. Not everybody gets off on that type of "excitement," and

2. There is no way I could hire someone else to do my job and train them on this method, which makes scaling on the "college senioritis plan" out of the question.

A while back, I had a conversation with a friend who had experienced the sudden departure of a valuable team member without much warning. Later on, I sent him an email, sharing my perspective on the significance of implementing effective systems and how apparent that would become at a time like this.

This weekend was the 1st anniversary of the day my Operations Director walked out on me. She was a close friend of 25 years, and when she left, she left violently. The week she left, I realized that I had made the mistake of trusting her with her work and expecting that if she ever left, she would honor our relationship in a way that allowed ample time for a transition that supported the company. That was not the case. She left without notice, and as I worked through the pain, I realized quickly that our processes were functional; However, none of it was documented, and to be honest, I was so busy developing other parts of the company that I didn't know how to do her job. So when my sister asked if there was anything that she could do to help, I was honest and told her, "I need a whole-ass Operations Director." I promoted her immediately, and together, we started to audit our processes and document them step-by-step. I then went on to do this in every department across the organization.

That was by far one of the most challenging periods in my life. But I learned that no one in my company should be the keyholder to information

I didn't have access to. I also knew that 80% of Black-owned businesses fail within the first 18 months for lack of sustainable systems, and even though, at the time, I was ready to give up and free myself, I know that God has tasked me with being the exception.

I believe wholeheartedly that you will be the exception. Because, in so many ways, you already are.

Transparent organizational Systems have the power to increase:

→   Efficiency

→   Accuracy

→   Effectiveness

→   Predictability

Increasing Efficiency

In today's fast-paced and competitive world, efficiency is a critical factor in the success of any organization. Organizational systems are the backbone of any industry, providing structure, clarity, and guidance for effective operations. In the ABA Industry, the implementation of organizational systems plays a crucial role in enhancing efficiency in several ways:

1.   *Streamlined Case Management:* ABA providers often work with multiple clients simultaneously, each with unique needs and

goals. Clear organizational systems help streamline case management by facilitating efficient intake procedures, scheduling client appointments, and managing treatment plans. By having standardized processes in place, ABA providers can optimize their time and resources, reducing administrative burdens and focusing more on delivering quality services.

2. *Effective Communication and Collaboration:* Communication and collaboration are vital in the ABA industry, as multiple stakeholders, such as clients, families, teachers, and healthcare professionals, often need to coordinate care for the best outcomes. Organizations must establish efficient communication channels, protocols, and documentation practices. For example, using centralized platforms for sharing information, such as client progress notes, treatment plans, and data analysis, ensures everyone involved can access the most up-to-date information. This streamlined communication improves coordination and minimizes delays, resulting in more efficient and effective interventions.

3. *Consistent Data Collection and Analysis:* Data collection and analysis are integral to ABA practice, as they inform decision-making and treatment adjustments. Documented organizational systems provide standardized protocols and tools for data collection, ensuring consistency across different cases

and practitioners. By establishing clear guidelines and expectations, organizations can reduce errors, improve data quality, and facilitate efficient analysis, leading to more accurate treatment plans and progress monitoring.

4. *Continuous Quality Improvement:* Well-designed systems serve as a framework for continuous quality improvement within the ABA industry. By implementing regular audits, performance evaluations, and feedback mechanisms, organizations can identify areas for improvement and continually refine their processes. By refine, I mean update them as often as necessary to ensure they are technological*. This iterative approach helps optimize efficiency by eliminating bottlenecks, resolving inefficiencies, and fostering a culture of learning and growth.

5. *Time and Resource Optimization:* Clear organizational systems allow ABA providers to optimize their time and resources effectively. By eliminating unnecessary administrative tasks, minimizing communication gaps, and maximizing the use of technology, organizations can focus on delivering quality services rather than getting caught up in inefficiencies. This, in turn, allows for increased productivity and improved resource allocation, ultimately leading to cost savings.

*Technological is one of the seven dimensions of Applied Behavior Analysis. It means that an intervention should be written in a manner that provides a clear and detailed description of all its components, enabling others to replicate it accurately.

Increasing Accuracy

Designing systems that are technological in nature results in improved accountability and compliance across the organization. During my 3rd year in business, I hired a business consultant to help me streamline the processes my team and I had already developed to improve our process fidelity. During our very first coaching session, this man, whom I paid to mind my business, asked me what I considered a "win" for the execution of any task or the output of any person in the company. I replied confidently, "I would be happy with 80-85% accuracy." He raised a brow, then went on to challenge my thinking: "Ok," he said casually, "I don't know if you've ever been on a plane or not, but what if a pilot announced over the speaker that he and all of his passengers had made it to his destination safely 85% of the time?" I immediately turned into the wide-eyed emoji. I couldn't muster an answer outside of, "I see what you did there. You're absolutely right."

I learned from him that day that I would only ever get out of my team what I expected from them. If I expected them to land at 80% accuracy in their roles and considered that a "win," I would build systems that produced only 80% of what was possible. Instead, if I set the standard at 100%, I would have to challenge myself to develop systems and tools that yield results ranging between 95%-105% of the goal. Immediately, this man showed me the secret sauce! I instantly understood on a deep level how Chick-Fil-a has managed to get their employees to say "my pleasure" in 100% of opportunities.

To take it further, healthcare organizations are often subject to various regulations, licensing requirements, and ethical guidelines. Transparent organizational systems ensure adherence to these standards by establishing clear documentation, record-keeping, and compliance monitoring processes. This minimizes the risk of legal and ethical violations and enhances the organization's reputation and credibility in the industry.

Increasing Effectiveness

Implementing transparent systems leads to more effective people management, which makes way for offering a more effective service delivery model. Well-designed organizational systems can facilitate evidence-based practices, ensuring that interventions are tailored to individual needs, resulting in better client outcomes. Team members at every level need well-defined roles and responsibilities. The ABA industry involves various professionals, including behavior analysts, therapists, and support staff. Clarifying roles and task-analyzing duties for each team member is a non-negotiable practice. It ensures a clear understanding of their assignments, expectations, and reporting structures. This clarity minimizes confusion and duplication of efforts, allowing individuals to work efficiently within their designated roles.

In addition, well-defined roles, efficient workflows, and clear expectations increase staff satisfaction. When team members understand their responsibilities and have the opportunity to conduct their work in an organized fashion, they are more likely to feel empowered and motivated. This increased job satisfaction improves overall employee morale and leads to better retention rates, reducing the costs and disruptions associated with high staff turnover.

Increasing Predictability

Implementing well-designed systems increases team members' ability to predict how effective they will be at completing a task, their next steps, how to plan for change, and how they may score on their performance reviews. In addition, leaders can yield more consistently favorable outcomes by making data-based decisions and predicting organizational outcomes as the business scales. As the demand for ABA services continues to grow, organizations with transparent operational systems are better equipped to scale their operations efficiently. With standardized procedures, established protocols, and effective communication channels, organizations can expand their services, onboard new staff, and handle increased caseloads without compromising quality or efficiency.

Operations, Defined

Before moving on, it's important to highlight the essential differences between four commonly used terms: systems, processes, workflows, and policies. These terms are interconnected but have distinct meanings and purposes within operations management. Understanding these distinctions can be helpful when managing and optimizing operations within an organization.

Systems

In the broadest sense, a system is a collection of interconnected and interdependent components working together to achieve a specific goal or purpose. Think about your company as a machine. Like any other, this machine has multiple parts, all with different yet equally important functions - the wheels of a car, the buttons on an ATM machine, and the operating system inside a computer. These are all examples of systems that drive the performance of the machine.

A system can be considered a comprehensive framework encompassing all the elements required to carry out a particular organizational function. It includes people, processes, technology, resources, and information, all operating harmoniously to achieve the desired outcomes. A system provides structure, integration, and coordination of various activities, facilitating efficient operations across different functional areas.

Processes

Processes are the series of interrelated steps or activities that transform inputs into outputs to deliver a product or service. They are the core building blocks of operations within a system. Processes can be viewed as a set of ordered tasks or actions, often involving the flow of materials, information, or both. Each process has its own objectives, inputs, activities, and outputs. They can be formalized through documentation, such as standard operating procedures (SOPs), and are subject to continuous improvement and optimization.

Processes can be categorized into three types:

A. *Management Processes:* These processes are responsible for governing and controlling the overall operation of an organization. Examples include strategic planning, budgeting, and performance management.

B. *Operational Processes:* These processes are directly involved in producing goods or delivering services. They focus on procurement, production, inventory management, and customer service.

C. *Supporting Processes:* These processes provide the necessary support to ensure the smooth functioning of the operational processes. They include activities like human resources management, IT support, and maintenance.

Workflows

Workflows refer to the sequential arrangement of tasks, activities, or steps required to complete a specific process or achieve a particular outcome. A workflow outlines the exact order, dependencies, and interactions between various tasks within a process. It provides a visual representation or a systematic description of how work should flow from one step to another, often involving multiple individuals or departments.

Workflows can be manual or automated, depending on the complexity and nature of the tasks involved. They enable organizations to streamline operations, identify bottlenecks, allocate resources efficiently, and ensure consistency in task execution.

Policies

Policies are guidelines, principles, or rules that define how an organization intends to operate or make decisions. They provide a decision-making framework and help establish an organization's boundaries and expectations. Policies serve as a reference point for employees, ensuring consistent behavior and actions aligned with the organization's objectives, values, and legal or regulatory requirements.

Policies can cover a wide range of areas, including human resources, finance, security, quality control, and environmental sustainability. They provide clarity and promote transparency in operations, enabling employees to understand their roles, rights, and responsibilities.

Here's a visual representation of how each of these terms feeds into one another:

RADICAL SYSTEMS

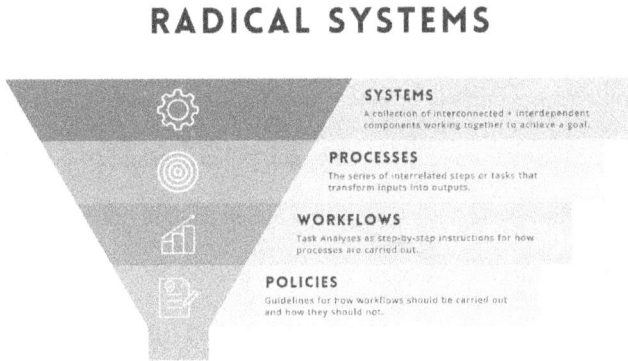

SYSTEMS
A collection of interconnected + interdependent components working together to achieve a goal.

PROCESSES
The series of interrelated steps or tasks that transform inputs into outputs.

WORKFLOWS
Task Analyses as step-by-step instructions for how processes are carried out.

POLICIES
Guidelines for how workflows should be carried out and how they should not.

Systems: The Intake Department is comprised of multiple processes related to the onboarding of a client.

Processes may include insurance eligibility verification, client onboarding, and functional behavioral assessment.

Workflows: The Client Onboarding workflow may be documented in the form of a checklist of steps to be completed every time a new client is onboarded. Steps may include collecting demographic information, scheduling the assessment, and submitting a request for authorization of services.

Policies are guidelines for how workflows should be carried out and how they should not. For example, a company may have a policy that states that a client's file will be closed following 3 attempts to contact the family without success during the intake process.

While the terms systems, processes, workflows, and policies are interconnected, they have distinct meanings and purposes within the field of operations management. Systems provide a holistic view of an organization's operations, processes are the operational building blocks, workflows illustrate task sequencing, and policies establish guidelines for decision-making and behavior. By understanding these differences, managers can effectively design, optimize, and control their organization's operations, improving efficiency, productivity, and customer satisfaction.

Chapter 6:
Radical Decisions

Do No Harm: A Four-Step Decision-Making Strategy For Leaders

In any organization, making sound decisions is a critical responsibility of executives. Every outcome, big or small, results from a decision, and decisions often lead to subsequent ones. For this reason, it is important to set policies that guide decision-making processes and establish clear criteria for when to delegate or defer decisions. By doing so, we can avoid or alleviate decision fatigue, promote efficiency, and ensure that important decisions are made with clarity and strategic foresight rather than emotion-driven impulsivity. Knowing when to leave well enough and avoid unnecessary decision-making can prevent burnout and allow executives to focus on high-impact choices that require our attention.

When faced with the challenge of scaling my business, the most difficult aspect was entrusting others to make high-quality decisions at a strategic level. As an entrepreneur, the pressure to make the right decision looms over me daily. I am acutely aware that decisions have far-reaching consequences that can impact the numerous stakeholders within my organization, numbering close to 300 individuals. Scaling my business necessitated teaching my management team the seemingly impossible task of thinking like me.

Initially, I believed I was effectively modeling decision-making through my interactions with the management team. I fantasized that one day, when it was time for them to take the reins, they would think back on everything I had taught them and that somehow, magically, they would feel confident in making high-level decisions. I also imagined that I would fully trust them to do this. However, through trial and error, I learned that I had been mistaken in my assumptions. Consequently, I went back to the drawing board and mapped out my approach to effective decision-making.

Assess the Need for a Decision

Consider whether a decision needs to be made. While this may seem obvious, many leaders frequently overlook this crucial step. Decision-making consumes significant time and energy at the executive level, which can be overwhelming even on the best days. While your team looks to you for guidance in making difficult decisions, teaching them how to define a problem and determine which issues warrant attention is equally important. This goes beyond mere prioritization and involves analyzing the available data:

→ What is the magnitude of the problem?

    ○ Is it a personal problem, a departmental problem or an organizational problem?

→ Who is impacted by this problem?

    ○ Is the problem internal or external?

    ○ Has anyone brought forth a complaint?

→ Is it a people problem or a process problem?

    ○ Is the problem a result of flawed thinking or a failure to adhere to an established policy or process?

    ○ Does a more significant problem exist that, if addressed, would subsequently resolve the current issue?

→ Lastly, what is the worst-case scenario if no decision is made?

Neglecting to consider the necessity of a decision can lead to unnecessary pressure, while making an unwarranted change may yield unfavorable results for stakeholders.

Make a list of all of the possible scenarios and outcomes.

Once you have determined that a decision indeed needs to be made, make a list of all of the possible outcomes. Include what will happen if you do nothing. In my experience, just about every decision has at least three possible consequences or outcomes. Consider the pros and cons of each option, as well as best- and worst-case scenarios.

You should also consider who will be impacted by the decision and what impact their reaction(s) may have on other stakeholders and, ultimately, the organization. Your team should know that some of the most incredible ideas may stem from the right intentions but come at the wrong time.

Eliminate options that do not align with the mission.

Staying focused on the mission is of paramount importance when making organizational decisions. An organization's mission serves as its guiding principle, outlining its purpose, values, and long-term objectives. It represents the core reason for its existence and provides a clear direction for all activities and decision-making processes. By staying focused on the mission, organizations ensure that their decisions are aligned with their overall goals and contribute to their ultimate success.

One key benefit of staying focused on the mission is the ability to prioritize effectively. Organizations face numerous choices and opportunities in a dynamic and fast-paced business environment. Without a clear mission as a reference point, decision-makers can quickly become overwhelmed or swayed by short-term gains. However, by constantly referring to the mission, they can evaluate options based on their potential to advance the organization's core purpose. This helps make informed decisions aligning with the organization's long-term vision, preventing distractions or deviations that may hinder progress.

As Behavior Genius started to grow, it became clear that as an organization and as a leader, my team and I had made several decisions that reflected our personal and professional values. Still, they needed to align with the organization's mission. For example, as a smaller start-up company, we offered snacks and meals to children receiving services in our treatment center. Due to our size at the time, ensuring that all staff were clear about each child's dietary needs wasn't impossible. In addition, I initially saw no issue with staff enjoying snacks and meals for themselves as well.

Things changed when my Operations and Finance team finalized our budget for the following year. Our purchase history data indicated that we were overspending on snacks and that, on multiple occasions, the person in charge of inventory had ordered snacks with allergens that we had prohibited in our clinic. Because they were part of a bulk order, they had made it past our approvals process. When management addressed these concerns with the team, they admitted that therapists had been allowing their clients more than one snack during therapy sessions. In addition to the snack issue, our landlord had received multiple complaints regarding baby wipes being flushed down the toilet, causing the pipes to clog. Our landlord began invoicing us for the damages because it had happened numerous times, resulting in hefty plumbing bills. This cost the organization several thousand dollars each year.

Initially, we decided to tackle these issues by updating a few related processes:

→ We updated our inventory SOP by adding approved shopping lists on Amazon so that the operations team had control over the type of snacks that were ordered;

→ We sent reminders to staff that each child should only be allowed one snack per day.

→ We notified staff and families that the company would no longer be providing diaper wipes or allowing diaper wipes to be utilized for children who were not in diapers.

Our team is comprised of some of the most empathetic and compassionate human beings on the planet. So, I'm sure you can imagine what happened next - *in came the complaints!* Soon after communicating the changes, I was informed that a few team members had raised concerns. The overarching question from the team was, *what about the families who cannot afford to send food or wipes with their child every day?* While I understood their intention in asking this question, I had to look at the situation from all sides. I began to compile my list of scenarios:

→ Do I care about the well-being of our clients? *Yes.*

→ Will treatment quality be impacted by this decision? *Not at all.*

→ If we move forward with this change, what is the best case scenario? *Cost savings. A program design that mimics the natural school environment, thus preparing caregivers and their children for generalization.*

→ If we *do not* implement the change, what's the worst that could happen? *Unexpected plumbing and grocery bills will continue to deplete our budget, resulting in a financial trade-off elsewhere. A child could have a severe allergic reaction while in our care due to a simple snack oversight, putting the company at a higher risk of a lawsuit.*

→ And finally - is the problem *mission-critical?*

Once I reached the last question, I realized the answer made all other questions obsolete. All I needed to know was *how this discussion relates to our mission of closing the gap in access to quality behavioral healthcare for the families we serve and how would making this change impact our one main objective - service delivery?* In essence, these additional expenses had nothing to do with our mission, nor did they serve to enhance the services that we provide.

And thus, my response became clear: *Our mission is not to provide food to children in underrepresented communities. There are other organizations that do serve that very important mission, and we would be happy to provide information regarding those resources to families who need them.* I can't tell you whether the team received that decision well. Still, it was clarifying and taught us an important lesson about decision-making at the organizational level: not every problem is our problem to solve. Eliminating these two unnecessary expenses allowed us to reallocate funds toward other places, such as planning an employee appreciation event or investing in software that would automate repetitive tasks. This would allow us to optimize multiple processes directly related to treatment quality across the organization, such as hiring, client intake, and scheduling.

Staying focused on the mission fosters consistency and coherence throughout the organization. When decisions are made in line with the mission, they reinforce the values and principles that define the organization's identity. This consistency enhances internal cohesion and aligns the efforts of employees, departments, and stakeholders toward a shared purpose. It also promotes a sense of trust and reliability among customers, partners, and investors, as they can rely on the organization to consistently deliver on its mission.

Furthermore, staying mission-focused enables organizations to adapt and navigate through challenges effectively. Inevitably, there will be obstacles and unexpected changes that require swift decision-making. By anchoring decisions to the mission, organizations can evaluate potential solutions based on their impact on the overarching goals. This enables them to make strategic choices that address immediate challenges and position the organization for long-term success. The mission acts as a compass, providing a consistent reference point amidst uncertainty and helping to guide decisions that will lead to positive outcomes.

In conclusion, honoring the company's mission is vital for making effective organizational decisions. It ensures that decisions are aligned with the organization's purpose and long-term objectives, facilitating prioritization, consistency, and adaptability. By constantly referring back to the mission, decision-makers can make informed choices that contribute to the overall success and sustainability of the organization. Embracing a mission-driven approach empowers organizations to stay true to their core values, inspire their employees, and build a strong foundation for growth and impact.

Opt for the decision that minimizes harm.

This is where you take the leap. It's time to make your decision. Begin by acknowledging that hardly any decision results in a win for everyone involved. Now that you have made your list of every possible outcome, select the one that does the least harm. "Harm" can encompass undue pressure or stress on certain team members, stretching the organization's financial resources, upsetting a substantial group of employees, or burdening individuals with excessive work for minimal or temporary results. When making your final decision, select the decision that poses the lowest risk possible and yields the highest potential reward.

Keep in mind that not all decisions are created equal. Some decisions may require taking higher risks to attain more significant rewards, such as moving to a larger office space in anticipation of a predictable hiring surge or establishing a new branch in a different location. In such cases, steps one and two remain crucial. This "do-no-harm" decision-making strategy is well-suited for day-to-day decisions in a fast-paced work environment. Moreover, it can be an effective teaching tool for emerging decision-makers within your organization.

By following this comprehensive decision-making approach, executives can enhance their ability to make sound choices and empower their management teams to do the same. Understanding the importance of assessing the need for a decision, considering various scenarios and outcomes, and prioritizing options that minimize harm can lead to more effective and informed decision-making processes. Leaders must impart these skills and methodologies to cultivate a culture of confident and responsible decision-making.

Ultimately, decision-making is a critical aspect of executive roles, and honing this skill is essential for success in driving organizational growth and achieving desired outcomes. By adopting a systematic and thoughtful approach, executives can navigate the complexities of decision-making, mitigate risks, and maximize rewards for the benefit of their organizations and stakeholders.

Radical Ethics

There is no conversation about decision-making without a discussion about ethics. Ethics in behavior analysis, leadership, and business ownership are critical in maintaining professional standards and promoting positive outcomes. Unfortunately, there are several super-common unethical practices within the industry that we are not talking about enough, although they need our collective attention.

Gatekeeping

Gatekeeping limits access to knowledge and resources within a particular field. In behavior analysis, gatekeeping occurs when professionals intentionally withhold or restrict sharing information, research findings, or resources that would otherwise help advance the understanding and application of behavior analysis. This can happen for various reasons, such as professional competition or a desire to maintain exclusivity within the field.

Gatekeeping is often apparent in conversations around hiring practices, hoarding information or ideas, or refusing to refer clients to other service providers who could meet their needs more quickly or effectively. By engaging in gatekeeping, these professionals hinder the dissemination of knowledge and impede the growth and progress of the science of behavior analysis. This behavior can limit opportunities for collaboration, innovation, and the development of new applications and techniques that could benefit practitioners and the individuals receiving behavior analytic services.

It is important to note that gatekeeping is generally considered detrimental to the field because it inhibits the open exchange of ideas and hinders the overall advancement of knowledge. Embracing a more inclusive and collaborative approach, where professionals actively share information and resources, fosters a healthier and more dynamic environment for the growth and dissemination of the science of behavior analysis.

Gatekeeping can have particular implications for black professionals in behavior analysis. Historically, certain professions, including behavior analysis, have faced diversity, equity, and inclusion challenges. Gate-keeping practices can exacerbate these challenges and create additional barriers for black professionals in several ways:

1. Limited access to opportunities: Gatekeeping can restrict access to critical resources, networks, and mentorship opportunities necessary for career advancement. Black professionals may face systemic biases and discrimination, making accessing these resources more difficult. When gatekeeping occurs, it can reinforce existing disparities and perpetuate underrepresentation within the field.

2. Underrepresentation in knowledge dissemination: Gatekeeping often involves controlling the flow of information, which can result in limited

representation of diverse perspectives and experiences. Minimizing representation involves failing to prioritize diverse voices and experiences, leading to a lack of inclusion and potentially perpetuating biases. By obstructing the dissemination of behavior analysis, professionals hinder knowledge sharing and impede the field's progress for professionals and the clients we serve.

3. Lack of role models and support: Gatekeeping, as it pertains to hiring, promotion, and professional development, limits the visibility of black professionals in leadership positions and influential roles. Lack of representation can impact aspiring black behavior analysts by limiting their access to role models and mentors who understand their unique experiences and can provide guidance and support. Black professionals may face additional challenges in navigating their careers and overcoming obstacles without these role models.

4. Impacts on cultural competency: Behavior analysis involves working with diverse populations, and cultural competence is essential for effective practice. Gatekeeping practices that restrict information sharing and resources can hinder the development of culturally competent and culturally responsive approaches within the field. This can result in inadequate understanding and application of behavior analytic principles in diverse communities, including those predominantly served by black professionals. This is dangerous for people in marginalized communities

since black minority professionals are typically the most competent, comfortable, and passionate about helping families in marginalized areas.

The Ethics Code set forth by the Behavior Analysis Certification Board calls ABA professionals to prioritize the best interests of our clients (section 3.01) by collaborating with colleagues both in and outside of our own professions (section 2.10) and consulting and referring to other providers (section 3.06).

Addressing gatekeeping in behavior analysis is crucial for fostering diversity, equity, and inclusion. It requires actively dismantling barriers, promoting inclusivity, and supporting the participation and advancement of professionals from all backgrounds. By embracing a more open and collaborative approach, the field can benefit from a broader range of perspectives, improve cultural competence, and ultimately enhance the impact of behavior analysis in diverse communities across the globe.

Systemic Racism and Fake-Ass DEI Initiatives

On May 25, 2020, an innocent black man was slaughtered in the street. The incident took place in Minneapolis, Minnesota, where George Floyd, a 46-year-old African American man, was killed in broad daylight while in police custody. George Floyd's murder gained widespread attention and sparked protests around the world. His death birthed a global movement against racial injustice and police brutality.

The encounter began when police responded to a call alleging that Floyd had used a counterfeit $20 bill. Officer Derek Chauvin, a white police officer, and three other officers arrived at the scene and attempted to arrest Floyd. During the arrest, Chauvin knelt on Floyd's neck for approximately nine minutes, despite Floyd's repeated pleas that he couldn't breathe. After several minutes of calling out for his deceased mother, Floyd eventually became unresponsive and was later pronounced dead at a local hospital.

The video footage of Floyd's arrest, captured by a bystander, went viral on social media, triggering outrage and widespread condemnation of the police department. The incident became a focal point for long-standing frustrations over racial profiling, excessive use of force, and systemic racism within law enforcement.

In response to George Floyd's death and the subsequent public outcry, numerous Diversity, Equity, and Inclusion (DEI) initiatives were launched nationwide. These initiatives aimed to address and combat systemic racism and promote equality and justice in the workplace and our nation.

But the workforce has fallen short.

There will be no change until we start holding ourselves, our colleagues, and our employers accountable to their messaging. When our people stopped marching in the streets, the pressure was off for the corporate effort. And consequently, what has happened is that white people have found yet another way to exploit and monetize the suffering of people of color, and we are drinking the Kool-Aid because, finally - *they see us.* Our people are so desperate to be seen that we are missing the reality of the situation:

They don't see us in positions of power.

They don't see us running our own companies.

They don't see us as partners in their companies.

They don't see us making decisions that impact their livelihoods.

They see us as tokens for their own benefit.

They see us as magnets for other people of color.

They are using a brutal, relentless, 200-year attack on our people as a marketing strategy.

And we are Ray Charles to their methods because it *feels* like progress for our suffering to be acknowledged.

Let me be the first to propose a worthwhile challenge to corporations across America (and I feel qualified to talk my shit on this topic because I employ over 180 staff members, and today, as I write this, 88% of them are people of color). In the words of the great philosopher and theologian of our time, Diddy, *"Send the receipts."*

Many corporations and organizations publicly expressed their commitment to DEI and racial justice. They pledged to promote diversity within their workforce, review hiring practices, and invest in programs that support underrepresented communities. Some companies also donated funds to organizations dedicated to racial equality and social justice causes. But in *real life*, post-pandemic hiring practices are still carried out in a way that makes it possible for a person of color to be an "only" at a company in a community that is approximately 65% Latino and 9% black.

We have an opportunity to use our influence in whatever way we choose. The Behavior Analyst Certification Board calls us to be culturally responsive (section 1.07), and diversity and representation are essential when delivering behavioral treatment services for several reasons:

Individualization: Each person seeking behavioral treatment services is unique, with their own set of experiences, needs, and goals. Effective representation ensures the treatment approach is tailored to the individual's circumstances. By understanding and considering the individual's background, culture, values, and preferences, the treatment can be personalized to maximize its effectiveness. This individualization promotes a better therapeutic alliance, increases engagement in treatment, and enhances overall outcomes.

Cultural Competence: People seeking behavioral treatment come from diverse cultural backgrounds. Cultural competence involves recognizing, understanding, and addressing the cultural factors that may influence an individual's behavior, beliefs, and attitudes. Practitioners can ensure appropriate and respectful interventions by incorporating cultural sensitivity and awareness into treatment. This includes considering factors such as language, religion, customs, and social norms, which can impact treatment adherence and engagement.

Access and Equity: Representation is crucial in addressing disparities in access to behavioral treatment services. Historically, specific populations have faced barriers to receiving adequate care due to systemic biases and discrimination. By having diverse and representative professionals within the field, it becomes more likely that individuals from underrepresented groups will have access to treatment providers who understand their unique needs and experiences. This can help reduce health disparities and promote equitable access to behavioral healthcare - which, for some of us, is 100% the reason we open companies, right?

Trust and Engagement: Representation builds trust and facilitates better communication between the provider and the individual receiving treatment. When individuals see professionals who look like them, share similar backgrounds, or have shared experiences, they may feel more comfortable and understood. This can enhance the therapeutic relationship, increase engagement in treatment, and improve treatment outcomes. Representation also helps challenge stereotypes and reduce the stigma of seeking behavioral treatment services.

Effective Communication: Effective representation enables communication between the provider and the individual. Language barriers, for example, can hinder the therapeutic process. Professionals who speak the same language or have language interpreters available can ensure accurate information exchange and understanding. Moreover, representation can also help address other communication nuances, such as non-verbal cues, cultural expressions, and idiomatic phrases, which can impact the effectiveness of treatment interventions.

These factors also impact employee well-being and retention, directly impacting service delivery. Organizations have an opportunity and a responsibility to develop a framework for auditing our processes, procedures, and practices for systemic racism and racial bias. Auditing your company's internal processes is vital for promoting diversity, equity, and inclusion. Here are three ways you can conduct such an audit:

1. Review your current practices to identify any potential biases or discriminatory elements.

Consider the following high-discrimination areas:

→ Hiring and recruitment: Examine whether your hiring practices promote diversity and inclusion, such as diverse candidate sourcing, unbiased job descriptions, diverse interview panels, and equitable evaluation criteria.

→ Promotion and advancement: Assess whether promotions and career advancement opportunities are offered fairly and without biases, ensuring all employees have equal access to growth opportunities.

→ Performance evaluation: Analyze your performance evaluation systems to ensure they are objective, transparent, and free from biases that may disproportionately affect certain groups.

→ Compensation and benefits: Review your compensation structures to identify potential wage gaps based on race or ethnicity. Ensure that benefits and rewards are distributed equitably among employees.

→ Complaint and grievance procedures: Evaluate the effectiveness and accessibility of your complaint and grievance procedures to ensure employees feel safe and empowered to report instances of racism or discrimination.

2. Conduct employee surveys and focus groups: Engage with your employees through anonymous surveys and focus groups to gather their experiences, perceptions, and suggestions regarding diversity, equity, and inclusion within the organization. Ask specific questions about any instances of racism they may have witnessed or experienced and their suggestions for improvement. This feedback will provide valuable insights into potential areas of systemic racism within the company.

3. Evaluate representation and inclusion metrics: Analyze data on representation and inclusion within your organization. This includes demographic information about your workforce, such as race and ethnicity,

at various levels and departments. Identify significant disparities or underrepresentation of certain groups, especially in leadership positions. Additionally, examine employee retention rates, engagement levels, and participation in training and development programs to assess if all employees are given equal opportunities to succeed and thrive. Ensure that the audit results are transparent for team members at all levels.

The impact of DEI initiatives has varied across different regions and institutions, and the work toward achieving meaningful and lasting change is ongoing. The murder of George Floyd served as a catalyst for a nationwide reckoning on issues of race and social justice, prompting conversations and actions that continue to shape efforts to address systemic inequality. Remember that auditing for systemic racism is an ongoing process that requires humility, collaboration, and a collective commitment to continuous improvement. It is important to involve diverse voices, including employees from marginalized groups, throughout the audit process to ensure a comprehensive and inclusive approach. Additionally, consider seeking external expertise from diversity consultants or organizations specializing in equity and inclusion to enhance the effectiveness of your audit.

Hold yourself and your team accountable for knowingly and unknowingly perpetuating emotional and mental violence toward people of color in the workplace. DEI efforts encompass embracing the diversity of thought and recognizing that different perspectives and approaches can enrich the field. By dismissing alternative viewpoints, professionals limit innovation and growth. This blocks visibility for new ideas and prevents the field from evolving in response to changing needs and challenges.

Unethical Transition

Disclaimer: There is no disclaimer. I take full responsibility for what I am about to say on this topic because it needs to be said. So, in the words of my good friend Crystal's (very unbothered) husband Ryan, *"If it don't apply, let it fly."*

For this conversation, we will refer to unethical transition from three different perspectives. I intend to shed light on how unethical transitions are perpetuated at all levels within our organizations in hopes that we can begin to reimagine how we conduct ourselves when our competing priorities interfere with our perceived ability to fulfill our ethical obligations.

Perspective 1: The Behavior Technician

For frontline employees, unethical transition comes by way of leaving a position without proper notice or consideration for the individuals impacted, such as families and clients. In other words, the "quiet quitting" and leaving without notice is giving "fuck these kids." This behavior demonstrates a lack of empathy and respect for those affected, suggesting that personal gain precedes professional responsibility. It erodes trust and damages relationships, which are vital for effective practice.

Now, I know what you're thinking. Perhaps you'd like to make the point that hopping from one company to another for higher pay or a professional development opportunity is necessary for your well-being. And you very well may be correct. In no universe should a person ever prioritize their company's needs over their own. However, when you take a position, both parties knowingly and unknowingly commit to a list of agreements that should seek to lead back to the well-being of the client as first and foremost, assuming that the client's well-being aligns with the values of the organization and the reason for your hire.

Take caution. Companies that pressure new hires to abandon their previous caseloads without notice call that same energy back to their organizations. This is a tell-tale sign that they have no regard for ethical transitions that serve the population and support client wellbeing. Their core intentions are to "plug and chug" - a term I learned from the Director of (National) Training and Development at a company I used to work for. Plug-and-chug as a strategy is not about quality or culture. Be careful not to sell your ethics for that extra dollar.

Furthermore, if you have been blessed enough to work for an organization that values its clients, they likely value you as well. Before jumping ship, try asking for a raise. One of the reasons for pay disparities for minorities and women is that white men over-inflate their value and then have the audacity to ask for what they believe they are worth. A client-centered approach to quitting involves exhausting your options for getting your needs met in your current role and, if that's not feasible, providing ample transition time that facilitates continuity of care as outlined in section 3.14 of the Ethics Code.

Perspective 2: The Behavior Analyst

One of the main job expectations of a Behavior Analyst is program design and development. Since client programs are individualized, it is not uncommon for Behavior Analysts to vary their own clinical practices to meet the needs of each individual client. Unfortunately, "meet the needs" also, at times, means that Behavior Analysts give more attention to the family than to the staff member or more attention to live training opportunities with the staff member than the administrative work of maintaining well-manicured programs. A good-enough Behavior Analyst will hold it all together, addressing the client's day-to-day needs and mentoring their team without issue. The problem arises when there is a change.

For example:

1. When the Behavior Technician turns over without notice, the child is suddenly left with no intervention.

2. When the Behavior Technician turns over with notice, but due to the lack of clear documentation and clean programming, the new team member requires the Behavior Analyst to be more present than usual to explain what's going on with the client program.

3. When the Behavior Analyst turns over, a new team member quickly becomes overwhelmed with rummaging through the bullshit to find any sign of program direction possible.

Knowing that turnover is inevitable in our field, Behavior Analysts can minimize distress for their clients, colleagues, and themselves by engaging in ethical programming practices. This may include maintaining clean, consistent, and uniform records across clients; performing regular audits to assess program quality; and increasing parent empowerment efforts so client progress is not halted entirely when expected or unexpected transitions occur. The truth is that I have seen the same impact to transition whether or not there was notice given because the programs are just not programmin' like they were in 2007. Behavior Analysts can't single-handedly control the market; However, if our programs were bullet-proof, not only would we be rendering higher quality services, but the threat of transition would lose its bite.

Perspective 3: The Organizational Practices

Business owners are not off the hook for this one! I told y'all about the plug-and-chug mentality that came straight from the top. This term was shared in conversations with directors across all departments, the Chief Clinical Officer, the CFO, and the CEO. No one challenged this mentality because it had been deemed necessary and appropriate for the continued financial success of the organization.

If the executive team had taken a different approach that pinpointed the underlying issues and was centered around better planning, they would have seen results beyond what they thought was possible. For example, given the very real contingencies that Behavior Technicians and Behavior Analysts face and considering how these contingencies impact program quality and effectiveness, especially during times of transition, organizations have got to get really clear on their succession plan and client transition strategy.

We can't guarantee the desired outcomes for these families, but we do have a responsibility to guarantee our efforts. As behavior scientists and data analysts, there is no excuse for perpetuating or overlooking poor planning for predictable changes. In fact, business leaders should be wildly meticulous about planning for the unknown at all times. And what we do, or fail to do, at the top trickles down and reflects our core ethical values. Front-line employees are not the only ones who can be bought. In fact, they're not even the first to leave their ethics up to circumstance.

Chapter 7:
Radical Change

Introduction to Change Management

Who loves change?? While change is the very thing that has kept me in the field of Behavior Analysis, most of the U.S. population would disagree. In fact, *one in three people would avoid change if they could.*

Change is a constant and unavoidable variable in the world we live in. *Especially now, post-pandemic.* For some, it's a time of uncertainty. For others, a time for innovation. Organizations, like living organisms, must adapt and evolve to thrive in a dynamic environment. This means that employees and entrepreneurs at every level have no choice but to learn the fundamental art of going with the flow and staying ready, so you ain't gotta get ready.

The statement itself emphasizes the importance of preparedness and being proactive. In every community, "staying ready" is associated with being alert, adaptable, and ready to face challenges or opportunities as they arise. The African American community has a long history of facing adversity, systemic challenges, and limited opportunities. In such contexts, being prepared and adaptable has been a survival strategy and a means to navigating some of the most challenging circumstances. We have watched our great-grandparents, grandparents, and parents adapt to some heavy shit. But while we may have it in the bag, navigating change is a whole 'nother ball game when leading a group of people.

As a formal discipline, change management has its roots in the mid-20th century. Before that, organizational change was often ad hoc, reactionary, and lacked a systematic approach. *Sound familiar?* People were, and still are, throwing balls in the air and faking it til they make it. While those methods may have gotten you this far, I can tell you from experience that they won't fly at the organizational level. Managing change continues to be a pressing concern for small businesses, especially in the ABA industry.

Between the summer of 2020 and 2023, I scaled my first company, Behavior Genius®, from 0-185 employees. As you can imagine, change was the only constant for my team and I. We changed processes, policies, and people. We even changed our mission, our vision, and our branding. As we continued to grow, we were forced to find ways to leverage technology, use systems that would meet our immediate needs, and scale with us to meet the ever-growing demand that this industry places on ABA companies. And for those who don't know, I'm not a techie - *I'm a Behavior Analyst.* Every time we implemented a new system across the organization, the most interesting phenomenon occurred - our team (about 10% millennials and 90% GenZers) struggled with implementation. Considering the fact that we are talking about 2 generations who were born into the age of computers, apps, and technology, my leadership team couldn't understand why the implementation of new technology, such as software and apps that would help them to navigate their roles more efficiently, was met with such overt trepidation. But, I understood it from a human perspective: they weren't resistant to learning something new; they were resistant to change. This was especially difficult for our team at a time when everything in our world was uncertain and constantly changing. During the COVID-19 pandemic, we were required to overextend our minds and nervous systems to protect our physical and mental well-being. Any additional labor beyond that was immediately rejected. For many of us, the lucky ones at least, work was the only stable thing we had. In essence, while every CEO in the nation honed in and mastered the art of pivoting, everyone else was just tired of navigating change.

The work of Kurt Lewin, a social psychologist, laid the foundation for change management. Lewin's three-step model - unfreeze, change, refreeze - introduced the idea of preparing individuals and organizations for change, implementing it, and stabilizing it. This model paved the way for subsequent change management theories and practices.

In the '80s, a renowned management consultant, John Kotter, introduced the eight-step model for leading change. Kotter emphasized the importance of establishing a sense of urgency, creating a guiding coalition, developing a vision, and empowering employees to act. His model highlighted the need for leadership involvement and effective communication throughout the change process.

Implementing effective change management strategies is crucial for organizations for several reasons:

1. Minimizing Resistance: Change often meets resistance from employees who are comfortable with the status quo. Organizations can anticipate and address resistance proactively by employing change management strategies and establishing buy-in with our teams. This helps minimize disruptions and enhances the overall success of the change initiative.

2. Maximizing Benefits and ROI: Change initiatives are typically driven by a desire to improve efficiency, productivity, and customer satisfaction or adapt to market dynamics. Effective change management ensures that these intended benefits are achieved and maximizes return on investment (ROI). By managing transitions effectively, organizations ensure process fidelity and can accelerate the realization of desired outcomes.

3. Enhancing Employee Engagement: Involving employees in the change process enhances their engagement and commitment to the organization's goals. As employers, we sometimes have no choice but to drive new initiatives, sometimes with ample notice and sometimes without it. But when it isn't possible to forewarn our team of what's to come, managing change with intention can make the team feel as though we are making the change with them instead of in spite of them. Just about anyone can appreciate the opportunity to be a part of something new, exciting, and necessary for growth. Change management strategies that emphasize participation, collaboration, and empowerment foster a sense of ownership among employees. This, in turn, leads to higher levels of motivation, productivity, and loyalty.

4. Mitigating Risks: Change introduces inherent risks and uncertainties. Poorly managed change initiatives can result in financial losses, decreased customer satisfaction, and negative impacts on organizational reputation. Internally, ineffective change increases employee frustration and manager exhaustion. Employing effective change management strategies helps identify, assess, and mitigate these risks, reducing the likelihood of adverse outcomes and increasing the chances of a smooth transition.

5. Building Change Capability: Change management is not a one-time event but an ongoing process in today's dynamic business landscape. By implementing effective change management strategies, organizations build their change capability. This includes developing a culture that embraces change, fosters trust between leaders and employees, and builds structures and processes that support future change initiatives.

6. Sustaining Organizational Resilience: Change is often driven by external factors such as technological advancements, market shifts, or regulatory changes. Organizations that can effectively manage change build resilience, allowing them to adapt and thrive in the face of uncertainty. As business owners, we must stay on the offensive end of our company's growth as much as possible, controlling what we can when we can. But also, it is necessary to be able to navigate having to pivot, sometimes suddenly, when unexpected industry changes arise. Change management strategies foster agility, flexibility, and a continuous improvement mindset, positioning organizations for long-term success.

Change management draws upon various disciplines, including psychology, sociology, organizational behavior, and business management. Some essential foundations of change management include:

1. Understanding Human Behavior: Change affects individuals within an organization, and understanding how people respond to change is critical. Factors such as fear, resistance, and the need for stability can impact the success of change initiatives. Even when implementing change management strategies, leaders should consider the psychological and emotional aspects of individuals undergoing change.

2. Organizational Culture: Every organization has its unique culture, which shapes its values, norms, and behaviors. Change management must align with the existing culture or consider cultural transformations to facilitate successful change. Cultural factors influence employee engagement, acceptance of change, and overall organizational change readiness.

3. Effective Communication: Communication plays a vital role in change management. Perhaps the most critical. Clear, timely, and transparent communication helps create awareness, manage expectations, and address concerns. Change leaders must craft compelling messages, utilize various communication channels, and actively listen to employees to ensure information flows effectively throughout the organization.

Change management has evolved as a critical discipline for organizations navigating the 21st-century workforce. By understanding its history, foundations, and the importance of effective strategies, leaders can embrace change as an *opportunity* rather than a disruption. Implementing robust change management practices empowers organizations to proactively manage change, engage employees, and achieve desired outcomes. In the next unit, we will explore the key components and a framework for change management, providing practical guidance for implementing successful change initiatives in your company.

Exploration

The first step in implementing a change is to understand the reason for the change and to determine whether or not a change is necessary. The intention of the Exploration Phase is to conduct a Root

Cause Analysis to pinpoint the scope of the problem or the opportunity. Questions to consider during this phase may include:

→ What problem are you solving?

→ Who is currently impacted by this problem?

→ Are there specific internal or external insights that could be used as data to justify the change?

→ What is the desired outcome of the change?

→ Who will be impacted by the change or lack thereof?

→ What is the current process, and is it ineffective, not being followed, or nonexistent?

→ What will happen if you do nothing at all?

A root cause analysis (RCA) is a systematic approach used to identify the underlying causes or factors contributing to a problem or event. It is a systematic investigation that aims to determine the primary reason or reasons behind an issue rather than just addressing its symptoms. Root cause analysis helps organizations understand the fundamental causes of problems, incidents, or failures, allowing them to develop effective solutions and prevent similar issues from occurring in the future. By first understanding the root cause, organizations can address the actual source of the problem rather than merely addressing its symptoms. This ensures that the change management strategies are targeted and focused on the right areas.

Root cause analysis also aids in effective decision-making and encourages a proactive approach to problem-solving. By understanding the root cause of a problem, organizations can take preventive measures to mitigate or eliminate the causes before problems arise. This minimizes the likelihood of recurring issues and promotes long-term success in change initiatives.

Implementing change management strategies involves introducing new processes, systems, or practices. By conducting a root cause analysis, leaders can identify inefficiencies and areas for improvement within their existing systems or workflows. This enables them to make necessary changes to optimize operations and achieve better results during the change process and beyond. Overall, root cause analysis enables organizations to address the fundamental causes of problems and implement successful and sustainable changes that are in the best interest of the organization and everyone inside of it.

Innovation

I'm just going to jump right into this one and say that, as a visionary, *Innovation* is my absolute favorite part of implementing any change. Being innovative taps into my natural creativity and instinctive need to be different and bring forth something the world has never seen. After pinpointing the problem and potentially also landing on a viable solution, it's time to put on your party pants and engage yourself and your team in the art of *operational design.*

Operational design is the systematic process of developing a clear plan and framework to implement a company-wide change. It involves analyzing the organization's current state, envisioning the desired future state, and outlining the necessary steps and actions to bridge the gap between the two. Here are some steps to designing a clear plan for implementing a company-wide change:

1. Define the Change Objective: Clearly articulate the purpose and objective of the change initiative. Identify the specific outcomes or goals the organization aims to achieve through the change.

2. Assess the Current State: Conduct a thorough assessment of the organization's current state, including its structure, processes, culture, and capabilities. Identify areas that need improvement or transformation to support the desired change. For example, consider what other Standard Operating Procedures must be updated to facilitate the change. If your proposed change will require a transition from one software to another, consider what departments will be impacted and how their teams' workflows will need to shift to accommodate the change.

3. Envision the Future State: Paint a clear picture of the desired future state after implementing the change. Define success, including the specific outcomes, benefits, and impacts on the organization, employees, customers, and other stakeholders. This is also an opportunity to review any barriers that may arise and how those will be mitigated. As much as the team should consider all of the possibilities, you should work together to address how negative impacts will undoubtedly be associated with the change. It's important to be clear and transparent with your team regarding what they will gain from the change, what will be lost, and why it is worth it.

4. Brain Dump: The next step is to brainstorm ideas. Write down all of the possible ways to bring about the change. For example, if you are evaluating a software change, do your due diligence. Schedule demonstrations for multiple competitors so that you have a well-rounded understanding of what is available and can make an informed decision on the best one. You should also jot down any ideas that may not require a significant change at all. For example, hiring another person in the department vs. leveraging technology or using AI to contact families to share a message via phone instead of email.

The purpose of this exercise is to evaluate the effort, risk, and impact of all of your options and use the process of elimination to determine the best path forward. A change that requires high risk or effort and has a low potential for positive impact may not be appropriate given other variables, such as the time it will take to implement the change or the team's current capacity for change, given other recent changes.

5. Identify Key Stakeholders: During the Exploration phase, you listed who would be impacted by the change or lack thereof. During this phase, it is important to refer back to that list and revise as needed. Stakeholders may include clients, staff, partners, vendors, etc. Understanding each stakeholder's needs and potential concerns will help your team to develop a strategy that strives to center them and proactively meet their needs and expectations.

6. Create a Change Management Plan: Develop a comprehensive change management plan that outlines the specific strategies, activities, and timeline for implementing the change. This plan should include communication strategies, training programs, resource allocation, and performance measurement mechanisms.

Timeline

Working backward from your launch date, draft a timeline to include team and client announcements, training, launch, systems integration, Q&A sessions, and a leadership team debrief. A timeline for implementing organizational change is essential for several reasons:

A timeline provides a structured framework that helps define clear objectives and milestones for the change initiative. It sets specific dates or time frames by which particular tasks or goals need to be accomplished. This clarity ensures that everyone involved understands the direction and purpose of the change, allowing progress to be measured and evaluated effectively. A timeline allows for better resource planning and allocation. By breaking down the change process into specific phases or stages, you can determine the resources needed at each step and allocate them accordingly. This helps avoid resource bottlenecks and ensures that the right people and materials are available when required, making the implementation process more efficient.

Furthermore, a timeline provides a structured approach to managing time during the change initiative. It helps create a sense of urgency and keeps the project on track by setting deadlines for various tasks. Having a timeline also promotes accountability, as team members know the timeframes and are responsible for meeting their deadlines. This increases productivity and reduces the risk of delays or procrastination.

Communication

A good communication strategy allows leaders to effectively communicate the change process, its timeline, and the expected outcomes to employees, customers, suppliers, and other relevant parties. Clear communication builds trust, manages expectations, and ensures that everyone understands the impact and benefits of the change. When developing your communication strategy, consider how the plan will be communicated to everyone at each level. I have made the mistake of providing a clear plan to my leadership team and assuming that the information would (1) trickle down so that even front-line employees were well-informed and (2) be delivered in the way that I would deliver it myself. This is not a safe assumption to make.

Before implementation, the team must establish buy-in at the leadership level by clearly articulating the reason(s) for the change, sharing the vision for the future and how the change aligns with that vision, and engaging your leadership team as influencers. Be clear on when and how managers should communicate the change across the organization at all levels. This information should be outlined in your timeline.

Effective change management has a lot to do with influence. Because the ultimate goal is to reach your intended outcome as quickly and smoothly as possible, and because you are one person, you will need to rely heavily on your managers to leverage their relationships with and influence over their teams to increase fidelity to the process. This means that not only is it imperative to clarify the team's messaging and provide the necessary tools when implementing a change, but it is equally essential to use extinction as a strategy to (abruptly) stop sending competing messages or permitting old actions that may interfere with the collective implementation of the new change.

For example, imagine that your organization has moved toward asking parents to communicate their need to cancel a therapy session using an electronic Cancellation Form. Doing so will simplify the cancellation process by streamlining communication and keeping the scheduling email inbox free of clutter. Ultimately, this change will result in fewer scheduling errors and less time wasted for the scheduling team, the clinical team, and the caregiver. This means more time focused on clinical quality vs.

administrative error corrections. Once the change is announced, the team continues to accept client cancellations via email, text, and phone calls. This increases the number of communication methods from three to four. The scheduling team now has to look for information regarding client cancellations in 4 different places. As new team members are onboarded, they are taught multiple methods for receiving communication regarding cancellations. Their workflows quickly become overwhelming, which leads to missed information, untimely communication, and frustration for the families and the Behavior Technician who have shown up for sessions only to be turned away at the door. Furthermore, the management team is unaware of which communication method was used and which should have been used and cannot give the pinpointed feedback necessary to resolve the issue and prevent future occurrences. The cycle continues in this way as a result of poor process fidelity.

A thorough communication strategy enables proactive risk management and contingency planning by building trust and reducing uncertainty. Organizations can increase the likelihood of successful adoption and long-term sustainability of the desired changes by identifying critical points in the change process, setting deadlines around adopting the change, and discontinuing the old procedures.

Measurement

When implementing organizational change, no matter how large or small, measurement can provide valuable insights and help assess the progress and impact of the change initiative. Using measurement as a strategy for implementing organizational change is especially helpful if you are a business owner or leader at a multi-level organization who needs to monitor the effectiveness of the change from an aerial view. By defining key performance indicators (KPIs) and setting measurable goals, you can objectively evaluate whether or not the change is producing the desired outcomes. Measurement provides data-driven insights into the impact of the change, allowing you and your team to make informed decisions and adjustments as necessary.

Measurement also promotes accountability and transparency during the change process. When specific metrics and targets are established, individuals and teams become accountable for their contributions to the change initiative. Transparent reporting and communication of progress against those metrics create a culture of responsibility and motivate individuals to align their efforts with the desired outcomes.

But wait - there's more! Measurement helps identify areas that require improvement or adjustment. By analyzing data and performance metrics, you can identify bottlenecks, inefficiencies, or areas where the change is not delivering the expected results. This information enables leaders to make data-driven decisions and implement corrective actions, ensuring that the change initiative stays on track and continues to drive positive outcomes. By continuously monitoring and measuring performance, you can identify opportunities for refinement and optimization. This iterative approach allows you to make ongoing adjustments and enhancements to the change process, ensuring its long-term success and adaptability to evolving needs and circumstances.

Furthermore, measurement provides tangible evidence of success, which is crucial for building confidence and gaining support. When you can demonstrate measurable improvements and positive outcomes resulting from the change, it reinforces the credibility of the change effort and builds trust among employees, stakeholders, and leadership. This, in turn, encourages continued commitment and investment in the change process for the current and future initiatives.

By now, I'm sure you're wondering *what* to measure. Organizational data works a lot like the measurement of client program data. Your measurement strategy should be clearly outlined from the initiative's beginning before implementation. The easiest way to determine what should be measured is to simplify your thinking: what is your intended outcome, and how will you know if you have achieved that outcome? For example, suppose your intended outcome is to reduce errors. In that case, your team should begin with baseline data on the number of errors per day before the implementation and continuously record the number of errors per day after the change's implementation. This also works for subjective quality measures, such as client or employee satisfaction scores.

If you already have a list of Key Performance Indicators (KPIs) related to your desired outcome, there is no need to develop additional measurements. Let's use the scenario from above and contract fulfillment as a KPI as an example: If a reduction in cancellation errors is intended to also increase opportunities for make-up sessions, it would be powerful to have post-change data that demonstrates an inverse relationship between the number of scheduling errors and the number of make-up sessions that are scheduled by caregivers.

Other metrics to consider may include:

→ Financial metrics such as cost savings, revenue growth, profitability, and return on investment

→ Operational metrics such as cycle time, productivity, quality, and customer satisfaction

→ Employee engagement and satisfaction via employee surveys, retention rates, absenteeism, employee participation, etc.

→ Consumer metrics such as client retention rates and customer complaints

→ Adoption and usage metrics for changes involving the implementation of new systems, technologies, or processes

→ Cultural and behavioral metrics (i.e., changes in employee behavior, collaboration levels, communication patterns, teamwork, and values alignment

It is important to note that the specific measurements will vary depending on the nature of the change and the organization's objectives. The key is to identify the metrics that align with the goals of the change initiative and provide your team with meaningful insights into its progress and impact.

Collaboration

Once a clear implementation plan has been drafted, it's time to assemble your change management team. To maximize creativity and diversity of thought, you should form a dedicated change management team with representatives from various departments and different backgrounds, skill sets, cultural perspectives, and experience levels. This team will drive the change initiative, communicate with stakeholders, and ensure smooth implementation. The purpose of the change management team is to establish buy-in at all levels, assist with reasonable delegation, foster a culture of shared control, and solicit feedback from stakeholders. Each member of the change management team should be able to contribute to the change initiative as follows:

Step 1: Establish Clear Communication Channels and Objectives

Effective collaboration during the implementation of organizational change begins with establishing clear communication channels and objectives. Change leaders should be expected to:

1. Clearly articulate the reasons behind the change, its intended outcomes, and how it aligns with the organization's vision and strategic objectives. This helps create a shared understanding among team members and stakeholders, fostering alignment and commitment.

2. Clearly define the roles and responsibilities of individuals and teams involved in the change initiative. Ensure that everyone understands their contribution to the overall effort and their specific deliverables and timelines. This clarity reduces confusion and promotes accountability.

3. Determine the appropriate communication channels for collaboration during the change process. This could include regular team meetings, digital collaboration platforms, email updates, or other forms of communication. Choose channels that facilitate open and transparent communication, enabling team members to share progress, challenges, and ideas.

Step 2: Foster a Collaborative Culture

This step involves:

1. Fostering an environment where team members feel comfortable sharing their ideas, concerns, and feedback. Leaders should encourage active listening and create opportunities for open dialogue and constructive discussions. This openness promotes collaboration and ensures that diverse perspectives are considered.

2. Promoting cross-functional collaboration by breaking down silos and encouraging collaboration across different teams and departments involved in the change initiative. Team leaders should be encouraged to facilitate cross-functional meetings or workshops where individuals can share knowledge, insights, and best practices. This cross-pollination of ideas enhances collaboration and promotes a holistic approach to change implementation.

3. Establishing ways to capture and share knowledge throughout the change process. This could include documenting lessons learned, creating a knowledge base, or organizing training sessions and workshops to disseminate expertise. Sharing knowledge facilitates collaboration by ensuring team members access relevant information and resources.

Step 3: Regularly Assess Progress and Adjust as Needed

Continuous assessment and adjustment are essential for effective collaboration during organizational change. Leaders and managers should be expected to:

1. Monitor progress: Regularly review and measure progress against the defined objectives and milestones. This could involve tracking key performance indicators (KPIs), conducting progress meetings, or using project management tools to monitor tasks and timelines. Regular monitoring provides insights into the overall progress and helps identify deviations or challenges.

2. Foster feedback and learning: Encourage team members to provide feedback on the collaboration process and share their insights and observations. Create a feedback loop that allows for continuous learning and improvement. Actively seek input on what is working well and what can be enhanced to strengthen collaboration and overcome obstacles.

3. Adapt and adjust: Based on the feedback and progress assessment, be open to making necessary adjustments to the collaboration process. This could involve refining communication strategies, reallocating resources, redefining roles, or modifying the collaboration channels. Being adaptable and responsive ensures that collaboration remains effective and aligned with the evolving needs of the change initiative.

By following this 3-step process, organizational change leaders can foster effective collaboration. Unlike the standard "train and hope" change management methods, this framework ensures that the information and messaging surrounding the change initiative remains consistent and is well communicated at all levels of the organization.

Implementation

...and FINALLY - It's time to put your strategy to the test. This is the step where you and your team stop talking about it and be about it. Being intentional about implementing an organizational change provides clear direction, optimizes resource allocation, engages stakeholders, mitigates risks, facilitates measurement and evaluation, supports long-term success, and enhances adaptability. It ensures that the change effort is purposeful, well-executed, and aligned with the organization's strategic objectives, increasing the likelihood of achieving the desired outcomes.

Communication

Once you have developed your communication strategy, create a clear and consistent communication funnel to inform all stakeholders about the upcoming change. Provide relevant information, address concerns, and highlight the benefits of the change. Regularly communicate updates and progress throughout the implementation process. In addition, your team should be informed of the chain of command for questions and concerns. If managers are unclear on the answers to their team's questions, they should avoid redirection and escalate the question to a peer or a change management team member.

Engagement

Engage employees early on in the change process. Foster a culture of openness and transparency, and actively involve employees in decision-making whenever possible. Address their concerns, provide training and support, and encourage active participation in the change initiative. At this phase, it is also important to have checks and balances in place to ensure that your training methods include all team members, regardless of their job title, tenure, or unique learning needs. Your change initiatives should be equitable and accessible to everyone required to adhere to them. Failure to provide adequate support to team members and consumers when changes arise can be perceived as dismissive or discriminatory and may result in higher frustration levels and breakdowns in process fidelity.

Execution

You and your team must execute the change according to the defined plan. Monitor progress, address challenges or roadblocks promptly, and make necessary adjustments. Ensure all departments and teams are aligned and working towards the change goals and milestones. Develop a fidelity checklist and audit the team's implementation of the change. Fidelity checks should be conducted more frequently in the beginning as a part of the team's training and support measures. They can fade as the team becomes familiar with the new process and execute the changes more accurately.

The leadership team should establish clear guidelines around performance management. Reinforcement and recognition should be provided for any team members who adopt the change, and corrective actions should be distributed to those who reject the change. This will ensure company-wide collective adherence to the change, thus yielding intended outcomes as quickly as possible.

Evaluation

Lastly, don't skip the part where you work with your team to evaluate and sustain the change. Your leadership team should be expected to provide you with the information you need to regularly assess the impact and effectiveness of the change initiative. Measure key performance indicators (KPIs) to determine if the desired outcomes are being achieved. Ensure all related policies, processes, and workflows are updated to align with the change and that those changes are shared at all levels. Continuously improve the change management processes and sustain the change by embedding it into the organization's culture and systems.

A good practice during and following any change is to survey your stakeholders to get a pulse on their experience and how they are coping with the change. The leadership team needs to know what went well and what didn't. It's also good to see how the change may impact the team's daily functions in ways you may not have considered. The change management team should ideally meet at the end of the launch week to discuss initial impressions, 14-21 days following the launch date to discuss any barriers or concerns that should be immediately addressed, and around the 30-day mark to review experience survey results and debrief as a team before closing out the project.

By following these steps, organizations can design a clear plan for implementing a company-wide change that considers stakeholders' needs, ensures effective communication, and maximizes the chances of a successful transformation.

Chapter 8:
Radical Leadership

Leadership plays a pivotal role in steering a team toward success. Effective leadership encompasses various styles, each offering unique perspectives and approaches. As organizations strive to achieve their vision and direction, defining and shaping leadership that aligns is imperative. However, a genuinely inclusive and adaptable organizational culture embraces different leadership styles whenever possible, recognizing that diverse leadership approaches can enhance creativity, collaboration, and innovation.

Leaders emerge in various forms within organizational behavior management, each exhibiting distinct characteristics and skill sets. Some leaders excel at strategic planning, charting a clear vision and direction for their organizations. Others possess exceptional interpersonal skills, nurturing strong relationships and fostering a sense of unity among team members. Some leaders thrive in dynamic and fast-paced environments, adept at making swift decisions and inspiring their teams to embrace change. By acknowledging and embracing these diverse leadership styles, organizations create an environment that encourages individuals to maximize their potential and contribute to collective success. Moreover, such an inclusive approach to leadership enhances organizational adaptability, equipping the organization to navigate through uncertainty and capitalize on emerging opportunities.

When evaluating the dynamics of a team, the impact of both effective and ineffective leadership is often equally far-reaching. The entire organizational ecosystem can suffer when leaders fail to provide clear direction, establish trust, and inspire their team members. Without effective leadership, team members may experience a lack of motivation, confusion about goals and expectations, and a diminished sense of purpose. This can lead to decreased productivity, increased employee turnover, and decreased overall team morale. Moreover, ineffective leadership can create a ripple effect, negatively influencing the organization's culture, communication channels, and the willingness of team members to collaborate and innovate. A lack of solid leadership can ultimately undermine the organization's ability to adapt to change, respond to challenges, and seize opportunities, making it vulnerable to internal dysfunction and stagnation.

Most business owners and executives build SWOT analyses that outline potential external threats to the business. The strategic focus is typically on factors such as the organization's competition, economic factors, legal issues, market demands, and financial constraints. In ABA, the competition is perceived to be high because there is an ABA company on every corner, and staff has the free will to hop from place to place at their leisure, resulting in high turnover and inconsistent service delivery. However, when we consider the market demand, the competition should be the least of our concerns. The biggest threat to any organization is a lack of effective leadership. It's the people inside of our organizations, in leadership roles, who can cause the most damage.

Leaders are tasked with the responsibility - and the freedom - to guide the culture and performance of an organization and all of the people inside of it. Influential leaders embrace the power of influence and choose whether to use their force for good or not. Leaders should be carefully examined by their character and selected for their positions based on their ability to lead themselves, others, and, eventually, the organization.

Leading the Self

Like a skilled navigator, a true leader must navigate through the uncharted territories of uncertainty, adapt to the ever-shifting winds of change, and harness the power of contingency planning to chart a course toward success. With each decision, we bear the weight of responsibility, understanding that our choices reverberate beyond ourselves, shaping the destinies of individuals and organizations alike. The contingencies of leadership demand a delicate balance of foresight and adaptability, requiring leaders to anticipate and prepare for multiple potential outcomes while staying nimble in the face of unforeseen circumstances. As we travel the path of leadership, we must master the art of strategic thinking, cultivating resilience, and embracing the unknown as an ally, for it is within the realm of uncertainty that the greatest triumphs and transformations often lie. In an industry where change is the only constant and where the ground beneath our feet may shift at any moment, leaders must embrace the challenges that come our way, viewing them not as impediments but as opportunities to transcend boundaries, inspire greatness, and forge a legacy that withstands the tests of time.

I remember the day my business coach casually asked me what it was like to build a company that scaled from 0 to over 100 employees in 2 years. *"Sharks."* I told him, *"I literally feel like I am swimming with sharks."* When I started my business, I was in the boat with my team, rowing alongside them. Then, that little sailboat grew into a larger ship with me as the captain, looking far enough forward to ensure the team could navigate the waters ahead. At about 100 employees, I felt forced into the water. As with any ocean, the water was cold and choppy. And I knew wholeheartedly that there were sharks in there. I didn't know where they were or how many surrounded me. I also didn't know if I was a proficient enough swimmer to weather the mass of what I had built. I woke up one day and realized I was no longer in the boat with my team. They were unable to see me, and in some ways, I believe that they felt as though I had abandoned them. I wished they did see me most days so they would know that I was treading water right alongside them, making way for a bigger impact than any of us had imagined. *"In essence,"* I told him, *"I feel isolated, misunderstood, and afraid."*

A few months after that conversation, post-professional identity crisis, a friend shared a quote I will never forget for as long as I live. It was a quote by Tony Robbins, and he asked, *"Who are you, uninterrupted?"*

The question itself was a tough pill for me to swallow because I was immediately triggered by the fact that I didn't know. I had spent nearly two decades trying to fit into people's narrow minds and, for the most part, succeeding. The vastness of my gifts and talents had never been permitted to flow *uninterrupted.* Being a black woman in a position of power demands an unspoken understanding that we will be only so much as tolerated on our *best days.* We are forced to make peace with being a walking oxymoron. Our survival depends on our ability to remain keenly aware of and responsive to how we are perceived.

We must be humble and confident, both champions and cheerleaders, unwavering in our craft, and flexible in our approach. We must establish boundaries but not come across as guarded. We must be decisive and objective, calculated and intentional at all times. We must be forward-thinkers; visionaries but stay grounded, focused, and yet present; direct and yet careful with our words. We must remember to bite our tongues but use our voices to encourage, empower, and inspire the uninspirable. *Superhuman.* But relatable and down to earth; think brilliant thoughts, but only speak when we are spoken to. And when they twist their knives, we don't dare bleed. We are conditioned to amuse them with our magic but forbidden from ever believing that we're the shit because it makes them uncomfortable when we celebrate ourselves without their validation.

Leading ourselves means knowing what empowers and makes us feel threatened. Because when our sense of self is tried by others, staying in the game requires courage and tests character. With every change in leadership within my company, it became increasingly clear that we all lead from such a vulnerable and personal place. And I've learned that whatever emotional healing has been ignored or gone unresolved will manifest in how we show up as leaders.

Leading Others

Understanding the intricate dynamics between leaders and their teams is vital to being an effective people manager. I have had the privilege and, at times, the challenge of working alongside various leaders throughout my career. Many of us, *especially black women,* have lacked adequate leadership and representation in leadership for our entire careers. Subsequently, we have been forced to shape our leadership style around the types of leaders we are striving *not to be.* In the spirit of analyzing human behavior, I will share some unspoken truths, shedding light on the impact of personal healing, or lack thereof, on leadership styles. It is crucial to recognize that leaders, like all individuals, carry our experiences and wounds, which inevitably shape how we show up in our roles. By examining these archetypes, we uncover the underlying connection between personal healing and leadership effectiveness.

The Non-confrontational Leader

One leader that often emerges within organizations is the non-confrontational leader. Despite a keen understanding of right and wrong, this individual remains silent, unwilling to rock the boat. They often sacrifice their own needs, their team's, and even the organization's well-being to maintain harmony. This pattern of behavior may stem from unresolved personal wounds related to assertiveness, conflict avoidance, or fear of rejection. The nonconfrontational leader's inability to address issues head-on hinders growth, stifles innovation, and perpetuates a culture of stagnation.

The Task-Master

In contrast to the non-confrontational leader, we encounter the task-master, a leader who diligently focuses on completing their to-do list. However, their struggle lies in prioritization. Burdened by their own unresolved challenges around time management or perfectionism, they become overwhelmed by a sea of tasks, failing to discern which holds actual value. Consequently, their team's potential remains untapped, as their focus remains solely on ticking off items rather than nurturing growth and development.

The Work Bestie

Everybody's BFF, motivated by a genuine desire for connection, often replicates patterns observed in their personal friendships within the workplace. Struggling to form authentic relationships outside of work, they seek solace in friendships with subordinates. Regardless of team performance, this leader hosts social gatherings and fosters an atmosphere where work and personal life intertwine. While this may initially create a sense of camaraderie, it can lead to blurred boundaries and favoritism and hinder professional growth and unbiased decision-making.

Furthermore, this person forgoes their commitment to the ethics code by turning a blind eye and knowingly overlooking poor performance even when it interferes with service delivery. They may also attempt to mitigate their team's poor performance by sharing in the work, burning themselves out. They relay information along with their opposing thoughts and feelings about the information and have no interest in presenting a united front with the organization. They will both intentionally and unintentionally drive a wedge between their team members and upper management, taking no accountability for their own lapses in communication.

The Reluctant Leader

Among the many leaders I have encountered, the reluctant leader stands out for their passive and avoidant demeanor. Often lacking the confidence to provide clear instructions or make decisive choices, they are caught in a cycle of indecisiveness. Their hesitancy may stem from a fear of failure, imposter syndrome, or past experiences that eroded their sense of agency. Unfortunately, this leadership style breeds uncertainty, delays progress, and creates frustration among team members.

The Trigger-Happy Leader

While some leaders struggle with passivity, others manifest their unresolved wounds through quick corrections and abrasive behavior. The trigger-happy leader, plagued by unresolved anger, triggers, or trauma, reacts swiftly and harshly to any perceived misstep. This leadership style erodes trust, demoralizes teams, and perpetuates a toxic work environment.

The One-Dimensional Leader

The one-dimensional leader clings to a single management approach in their quest for stability or control. Unwilling to adapt or meet people where they are, they impose their rigid style upon diverse teams.

This inability to flex inhibits collaboration, stifles creativity, and impedes progress. Often, this leader's resistance to change stems from their own inability to take the perspectives of others or deeply rooted patterns ingrained in their personal journey.

The Savior

Sometimes, we encounter leaders driven more by personal significance than their team and organization's collective growth and well-being. The savior seeks to establish themselves as the indispensable figure, craving recognition and validation. However, their focus on their own significance diminishes their ability to empower and engage their team in meaningful work. Their personal healing requires constant praise and affirmation, so they go out of their way to be everything to and for everyone, then feel underutilized and undervalued if they can't have their hands in every part of the organization. They pride themselves on "standing in the gap" and genuinely believe they are the reason the team is intact. If the culture takes a dive, they will also believe that they are the ones who can turn it around.

The savior also acts as a bottleneck, embodying a micromanaging and controlling style. Deep-rooted insecurities, fear of failure, or a need for certainty drive their actions. This leader leaves no room for autonomy or discretionary decision-making, demanding constant oversight and approval.

Team members become prompt-dependent, afraid to make mistakes, and innovation suffers as a result.

The People-Pleaser

In our exploration of leadership archetypes shaped by personal healing, we must not overlook the presence of the people-pleaser. Driven by an inherent desire to gain approval and acceptance, this leader finds themselves entangled in a web of pleasing others at the expense of their own needs, the team's objectives, and even the organization's best interests.

The people-pleaser's underlying wounds may stem from experiences of rejection, fear of criticism, or a deep-seated need to be liked. This often leads them to prioritize the comfort and happiness of others above all else, regardless of the impact on the team's performance or the achievement of organizational goals. They tend to suppress their voice and delay bringing forth significant concerns or necessary feedback.

While the intentions of the people-pleaser are rooted in empathy and a genuine desire for positive relationships, their leadership style can have unintended consequences. By constantly striving to please everyone, they risk diluting their authenticity and compromising their ability to make difficult decisions.

Furthermore, the people-pleaser may inadvertently create an environment where mediocrity is tolerated, as they may be reluctant to hold team members accountable or address underperformance. Their avoidance of necessary confrontation can stifle growth, inhibit innovation, and limit the team's potential. It can also mean that unacceptable behaviors and actions are tolerated for far too long, potentially causing damage to other team members.

To break free from the people-pleasing cycle, personal healing becomes paramount. The leader must confront their fears of rejection and develop a deeper understanding of their needs and values. Building assertiveness and cultivating self-confidence can enable them to strike a balance between meeting the needs of their team and upholding their responsibilities as a leader. They must learn to prioritize the organization's objectives and make decisions that may not always please everyone but are in the best interest of the team and the greater vision.

Leaders can transform their leadership style by recognizing and addressing their own wounds. They can foster open communication, constructive feedback, and accountability, empowering their team members to grow, excel, and contribute to the organization's success. By healing themselves, they become better equipped to lead with authenticity, purpose, and a focus on collective well-being.

By shedding light on different leadership archetypes, we uncover the importance of personal healing and growth in fostering effective and impactful leadership. Leaders must embark on their own healing journeys, address their wounds, and seek personal growth. Only then can they transcend their limitations and create a nurturing, empowering environment where individuals and organizations thrive.

Leading the Organization

Leading an organization with intention is of utmost importance as it sets the direction and purpose for the entire entity. When leaders operate with intent, they possess a clear vision, a well-defined strategy, and a deep understanding of the organization's values. This approach enables them to make informed decisions, prioritize effectively, and inspire others to achieve a common goal. However, leading an organization differs significantly from leading oneself or other individuals. While leading the self requires self-awareness, self-motivation, and personal accountability, leading others demands strong interpersonal skills, empathy, and the ability to foster collaboration. Leading an organization necessitates additional skills, such as strategic thinking, organizational design, and the capacity to manage complexity. The leader must navigate diverse stakeholder interests, align teams, and create an environment that encourages innovation, adaptability, and growth. Understanding these differences not only shapes the organization's success but also empowers individuals within it to reach their full potential.

Leading an organization will likely be the most formidable challenge of your career. I can only speak from my own experience. The intersectionality of race and gender significantly shapes the experiences of

Black women who lead organizations, making it that much more challenging to do so. It is essential to acknowledge that while Black women have made significant strides in breaking through glass ceilings, systemic barriers still exist. According to the Center for American Progress, as of 2021, Black women held just 1.6% of executive or senior-level positions in S&P 500 companies, highlighting the persistent underrepresentation in leadership roles. Despite this, black women have continued to serve as pioneers, forging a way out of corporations where we have been overlooked and creating our own opportunities.

Black female executives face many stereotypes and biases that influence perceptions of our competence, authority, and capabilities. And unfortunately, these issues are amplified in entrepreneurship. Black female business owners continue to be among the most disrespected of all CEOs. To weather the storm and eventually find ourselves on the other side of the things that have held us back for generations, we must seek to become radical leaders and encourage others to follow in our footsteps.

Radical leadership, also known as transformative or revolutionary leadership, involves a style of leadership that challenges and disrupts existing norms, systems, and structures in pursuit of significant change. It goes beyond incremental improvements and seeks to create transformative and profound shifts in organizations, societies, or movements. Radical leaders aim to inspire and mobilize others to challenge the status quo and pursue a vision of radical change.

Key characteristics of radical leadership include:

Visionary Thinking: Radical leaders have a clear and compelling vision for the future. They envision a radically different and improved reality and communicate this vision with passion and conviction. They inspire others to pursue this vision and challenge the existing paradigms.

Courage and Risk-Taking: Radical leaders are willing to challenge established norms and power structures. They are not afraid to confront adversity, opposition, or criticism in pursuing their goals. They exhibit courage and resilience, even in the face of significant resistance.

Empowerment and Inclusion: Radical leaders empower others to be agents of change. They create an inclusive and participatory environment where individuals feel empowered to contribute their ideas, perspectives, and talents. They foster collaboration, diversity, and collective ownership to drive radical change.

Mobilization and Activism: Radical leaders are skilled mobilizers and activists. They engage in grassroots organizing, activism, and advocacy to mobilize support, raise awareness, and effect change. They inspire people to take action and challenge the systems and structures perpetuating inequality, injustice, or other societal issues impacting our organizations.

Ethical and Values-Driven: Radical leaders are guided by a strong sense of ethics and values. They operate with integrity, authenticity, and a commitment to social justice. They prioritize equity, fairness, and inclusivity in pursuing radical change and hold themselves and others accountable to these values.

Systems Thinking: Radical leaders take a systemic approach to change. They analyze and understand the underlying structures, policies, and power dynamics that contribute to the issues they seek to address. They seek to transform the root causes of problems rather than merely managing symptoms.

Radical leadership can take different forms and be applied in various contexts. It is often associated with movements for social justice, political change, or organizational transformation. People of color are constantly navigating all 3 contexts just by existing in the workforce. Radical leaders challenge conventional wisdom and push the boundaries of what is possible, driving significant shifts in beliefs, practices, and cultural norms.

Next Up: *Leading an Industry.*

(Because are we ever satisfied?)

Chapter 9:
Radical Performance

PART ONE: ORGANIZATIONAL PERFORMANCE

"To be a proactive manager, you must define the results that you need and then determine the behaviors that will produce those results." -Aubrey Daniels, Performance Management

During my third year in business, my team and I set out to start a movement. After spending nearly two years feeling helpless and unworthy of leading a team of such magnitude, let alone a movement, I guess I finally got tired of my own shit.

For two years, I had felt as though I was falling short. I didn't start off with a clear long-term vision for my company. I was running away from 14 years of workplace trauma when I started my entrepreneurial journey. I had made a vow that I would never find myself in a vulnerable position again. That I would never be silenced or taken for granted. That I would never again be disrespected in the ways I had been disrespected in my past. This was a self-fulfilling prophecy because when we focus on our fears, we build replicas of those exact things.

Entrepreneurship has granted me more freedom than ever, but not necessarily more joy. I remember feeling particularly out of control one day, and I sat at my desk, shrugged my shoulders, and said, "You know what, God? This is *your* business. So whatever you wanna do, you gon' have to do it." After that, I went on about my day. *And everything changed.*

I started to get really clear on my "big hairy-ass goals." My thinking sharpened. My intuition spoke more clearly than it ever had. And I knew that all I had to do was *lean in.* I realized that for 2 of my 3 years in business, I had been grappling with the idea that I had built this machine and that, at 184 employees, it had grown beyond my control. It was as if I had gotten onto this spaceship, people got on with me, and as we journeyed together through the unknown, more and more people boarded the ship. At different points, people tried to take over and fly the ship. And if I'm being completely honest, after a while, I gave up and let them have it. I didn't like what I had built. I sat back and said to myself and others, "After a while, it outgrows you. There are too many people. I no longer have control." I felt as though I had birthed the 21st-century Frankenstein.

In my mind, my garden had overgrown, and I had no experience pruning it and restoring it to its intended purpose. I was tired of swimming against the current. My focus was so clouded that I didn't see the light at the end of the tunnel anyway. *So run it into the ground if that's what y'all gon' do, and maybe you'll learn your lesson. And perhaps that's the purpose of it all.* And that's what they did. They didn't have the power to run it into the ground. But they damaged what they could and took hostages. And several of those hostages went out into the deep and came right back. And that's when I realized that even when I felt like all had been lost, we were still outperforming other companies like ours just by having the courage to be different, even if we weren't perfect. And I learned that the right people - the people who belonged on the ship, would realize that without coercion.

I had been perpetuating a narrative I had heard from other CEOs in my industry. And that narrative was reinforced by other industry leaders. I had danced one too many times with the idea of believing that this was just the way it was. Not once did I put on my BCBA hat. I wasn't thinking about my own track record, brilliance, and willingness to be creative and faithful enough to believe that I could do something that no one's ever done. I didn't feel that with everything going on around me, I could shift an entire culture. I had stopped believing in my gift of influence. My vision was short-sighted because I lost focus. And when I lost focus, I lost *hope.*

And when I lost hope, I began to lose *heart.* I struggled to see myself and my team on the other side.

Determined not to give up just shy of a potential victory, I started moving more quickly and deliberately toward the type of freedom and peace I needed to keep running the race for myself and everyone who would come after me. I feared that I would gas out before arriving at whatever destination God had for me. Hence why I'm so intense and intentional all the time (and efficient). And this was a growth opportunity for me. A difficult challenge. Because I knew wholeheartedly that I would never get there without people. And for my entire career, it has been so much easier navigating my own personal and professional barriers, slaying my own dragons, and controlling my own performance.

So, I did what any other self-respecting millennial entrepreneur-slash-behavior scientist would do and gave myself a 90-day challenge. I set out to use the principles of Organizational Behavior Management to transform my company's culture and, eventually, my industry. My desired outcome was to reduce the perpetuation of "hustle culture" and subsequently increase productivity.

I told my husband what I wanted more than anything: to change the narrative for myself and everyone who had ever felt this helpless in their business. My husband is a man of few words, so I shared this vision with him and asked him what he thought. And he said that there's a quote that he heard, and it's straightforward: "Winners Win." He reminded me of how certain people are destined to win and overcome. And no matter their circumstances or what crosses their path, people like that win because they are wired and determined to do so. So the following week, I called in my change-makers, and together, we built a radical framework and staged an intervention.

Pinpointing Your Desired Outcome

The secret sauce for broad organizational change is **Singleness of Purpose.** Pinpointing your desired outcome is paramount when attempting to effect organizational change as a leader or business owner. Everyone, at every level, needs to see the target. Without a clear vision of the intended destination, the journey becomes aimless and lacks direction. By defining your desired outcome, you set a strategic course for your company, aligning efforts and resources toward a specific goal. This clarity empowers you to make informed decisions, communicate effectively with your team, and chart a path forward. Pinpointing the desired outcome also serves as a powerful motivational tool, igniting enthusiasm and commitment within the organization. It creates a sense of purpose and direction, fostering a collective drive toward success. Moreover, by precisely identifying the desired outcome, you can measure progress and evaluate the effectiveness of your actions, enabling you to make necessary adjustments and stay on track. Ultimately, the ability to pinpoint your desired outcome provides the foundation for effective leadership and ensures that organizational change efforts are purposeful, impactful, and aligned with long-term success.

When you clearly articulate the desired outcome, it becomes a rallying point for your employees, enabling them to understand and embrace the purpose behind the change initiatives. This shared understanding fosters a sense of unity and collaboration, propelling the organization forward with a shared sense of direction.

Furthermore, a clearly defined desired outcome empowers you as a leader or business owner to make strategic decisions that align with your vision. It provides a filter through which you can assess various options and choose the most effective path to achieve your goals. With a laser-like focus on the desired outcome, you can prioritize tasks, allocate resources, and establish milestones that contribute to its realization. This targeted approach enhances efficiency and minimizes wasted effort, ensuring your organization remains on track during the change process.

Moreover, the ability to pinpoint your desired outcome allows you to effectively communicate your vision to stakeholders both within and outside the organization. By articulating the desired result with clarity and conviction, you inspire confidence and build trust among your employees, customers, investors, and other key stakeholders. This shared understanding helps to align expectations and gain support for the change initiatives, fostering a positive environment that encourages collaboration and engagement.

Pinpointing the desired outcome also provides a basis for measuring progress and evaluating the success of your change efforts. By setting specific, measurable, attainable, relevant, and time-bound (SMART) goals that align with the desired outcome, you create a framework for tracking performance and monitoring the impact of your actions. This allows you to identify areas of improvement, celebrate milestones, and make informed adjustments along the way. Regularly assessing progress against the desired outcome helps you stay agile and responsive, adapting your strategies to achieve the desired results.

Pinpointing Specific Employee Behaviors Needed to Ensure Success

Identifying specific employee behaviors is the most effective way to drive the success of a project or change. Clarifying desired and undesired behaviors sets clear expectations and standards for employees, providing them with a roadmap for success. Leaders can align their team's efforts toward a common goal by defining and communicating the specific behaviors necessary to achieve the desired outcomes. This approach promotes consistency, accountability, and a shared understanding of the required actions, fostering a culture of ownership and commitment among employees. Pinpointing specific behaviors also enables leaders to provide targeted feedback, coaching, and recognition, facilitating individual and team growth. Ultimately, leaders can effectively guide their organizations through change and project implementation by focusing on the behaviors that drive success, maximizing the chances of achieving desired outcomes.

In addition to setting clear expectations and standards, defining target employee behaviors as key performance indicators provides a framework for measuring progress and performance. When leaders can identify and describe the behaviors that contribute to project success, they can track and assess the extent to which employees demonstrate those behaviors. This enables leaders to monitor the effectiveness of their change efforts and make data-driven decisions to adjust strategies if needed.

Moving in this way helps to create a culture of transparency and accountability within the organization. When employees understand the behaviors essential for achieving success, they become more aware of their individual contributions and impact on the overall outcome. This awareness fosters employees' sense of responsibility and ownership, motivating them to align their actions with the desired behaviors. By holding individuals accountable for their performance and behaviors, leaders can ensure everyone actively works towards the same goals and objectives.

Furthermore, by focusing on specific behaviors, leaders can provide targeted training and development opportunities to help employees acquire the necessary skills and competencies. This approach allows leaders to address any gaps in knowledge or capabilities that may hinder the success of the project or change initiative. By investing in employee growth and development, leaders can empower their teams with the tools and resources needed to excel in their roles, ultimately driving organizational success.

Pinpointing Barriers to the Outcome

Identifying and understanding barriers to the success of a project allows for strategic planning, effective decision-making, and the implementation of targeted solutions. By addressing the obstacles that impede progress, leaders can pave the way for successful change initiatives and ensure their organizations' long-term growth and sustainability.

Here are some key reasons why identifying and resolving barriers is essential for affecting organizational change:

1. Accurate assessment: Knowing your barriers enables leaders to assess the situation thoroughly and accurately. This involves identifying the specific challenges, roadblocks, and resistance that hinders progress. Without a clear understanding of these barriers, leaders risk implementing change initiatives that fail to address the root causes of organizational inefficiencies.

2. Strategic planning: Pinpointing barriers helps leaders develop a strategic plan to overcome them. It allows them to prioritize resources, allocate budgets, and design tailored solutions directly targeting the identified obstacles. By aligning the change efforts with the specific barriers, leaders can optimize their strategies and increase the chances of success.

3. Stakeholder engagement: Understanding the barriers to success facilitates effective stakeholder engagement. Different individuals or groups within an organization may have varying perspectives and concerns about the proposed changes. By identifying and addressing their specific problems, leaders can foster buy-in, collaboration, and stakeholder support, increasing the likelihood of successful change implementation.

4. Risk mitigation: Pinpointing barriers helps leaders assess potential risks and mitigate them. Change initiatives often come with uncertainties and risks that can derail progress. By identifying and analyzing potential obstacles, leaders can proactively develop contingency plans and risk management strategies to minimize the negative impact of these barriers on the change process.

5. Resource optimization: Addressing barriers allows leaders to optimize the utilization of resources. By understanding the specific challenges that need to be addressed, leaders can allocate resources more efficiently, ensuring that investments in the change process are strategically focused and yield the desired outcomes.

6. Continuous improvement: Identifying barriers to success is a stepping stone toward continuous improvement. By recognizing and addressing obstacles, leaders create a culture of learning and adaptability within the organization. This mindset encourages ongoing evaluation, feedback, and adjustment, enabling the organization to continuously evolve and thrive in a dynamic business environment.

People, especially in the workplace, thrive on predictability. In fact, the ultimate win for any Behavior Analyst is to find areas of predictability and use that predictability to drive observable and measurable change. Predictability is paramount when running a company and implementing organizational change initiatives. It provides stability and direction, enabling leaders to make informed decisions and employees to work effectively. Predictability creates a cohesive environment, fostering trust and confidence among stakeholders. It minimizes uncertainty and maximizes efficiency. By improving predictability, companies can adapt to change more smoothly, navigate challenges with resilience, and sustain long-term growth.

Furthermore, when an organization achieves a higher level of predictability, it results in increased employee compliance, improved fidelity, and greater, more sustainable outcomes.

PART TWO: INDIVIDUAL PERFORMANCE

Pinpointing for Performance

At almost every company I have ever worked for, heard of, or seen on Netflix, improving employee productivity emphasizes the importance of clear and consistent consequences. These are typically harmful consequences that, over time, break spirits and limit creativity.

171

When evaluating employee performance, there are factors beyond the performance itself that should be considered:

Are the expectations of the organization clearly defined?

Does the person have the proper skills, tools, and support?

Is the person lazy, or do they lack confidence?

Is their poor performance being inadvertently reinforced?

Are they neurodivergent (diagnosed or undiagnosed)?

Is the problem that they are passive, or are they having difficulty making decisions?

What are they thinking about, and what should they be thinking about instead?

Leaders create better synergy among their teams by pinpointing reasons for undesired performance. Synergy refers to the characteristic of a system, process, or relationship where the combined effect of the elements or components is greater than the sum of their individual effects. In a synergistic scenario, the elements or components work together harmoniously, enhancing each other's capabilities and producing superior or more impactful results than what could be achieved in isolation.

A thorough evaluation of performance requires a deeper dive and a genuine interest on behalf of the leader in clarifying the target, developing the person, excavating their gifts, and honing their capabilities. The idea of pinpointing is essential here too! Imagine that you have been working with someone whose performance has yet to impress you. You've modeled the desired behavior and provided clear feedback. And no matter what support you have put in place, you cannot get the person to execute the mission. They have the skill and a clear understanding of the target. They understand exactly how their performance (or lack thereof) ties back to the mission and vision of the organization. You are frustrated AF. But here's another perspective: Perhaps the skill to teach or the feedback to give is not about the work itself; instead, this person requires additional training and support to make quicker or more strategic decisions. Maybe this person wants to honor deadlines, but they have become an advocate for their team and have taken on an invisible workload - jumping in to keep the team from feeling overwhelmed. Maybe they are more focused on putting out fires than on preventing them. These are skills that can be taught and barriers to performance that should be considered.

There is power in being the type of leader who taps into the individualized needs of your team members. At a time when the workforce is so fragile, and an unconditional work ethic is hard to come by, we should change the way that we evaluate effort. We can all appreciate the effort. However, effort doesn't carry empires - *effectiveness does.*

A framework for evaluating barriers to employee effectiveness will help you and your team maximize your team's performance while automatically weeding out anyone whose efforts don't align with the vision.

Competence

Having employee competencies clearly defined for every position in an organization is the first step to improving employee performance. We all need an operational definition of our job expectations. I remember being assigned a problem to fix. The CEO of the company I worked for said, "I don't care how you do it, just get it done." So, I got it done. And when the other directors and I presented the results of our project, she listened quietly to the entire presentation before saying, in the most dismissive way possible, "I don't want to use the word 'trash,' but you completely missed the mark."

My mouth and my heart dropped. And my peers and I sat quietly for the rest of the meeting, trying to figure out where we had gone wrong and how we would fix it. And even worse, what if we tried to fix it and still fell short? It was as though she enjoyed watching us jump through the hoops. At the end of the conversation, I nervously raised my hand: "Do you have a specific way you would like this to be executed? You gave us a blank canvas. But if you gave us a target, we would have hit it. *I don't miss.*"

If you're reading this and think this woman believes in setting people up for success, lower your expectations. She didn't offer any direction, and at the time, I thought it was because she wanted to challenge us in some way or teach us something. But I realized soon after that incident that her approach reflected her competence, not ours.

Written competencies serve as a comprehensive framework that outlines the skills, knowledge, and abilities required for successful job performance. They demonstrate to the performer that you, as a leader, know precisely what you're looking to accomplish and the steps it takes to make it happen. Instead of leaving the *how* up to interpretation, it lays a clear foundation for optional performance and is a supportive guide for the employee.

People also like to know whether they are off track and when they're killin' it. Competencies give managers a framework to evaluate their team's performance fairly and objectively. Organizations can align their recruitment, selection, and training processes by clearly articulating the expected competencies. Having well-defined competencies ensures that employees possess the necessary qualifications and capabilities to perform their roles effectively. It also aids in setting performance expectations, designing professional development programs, and conducting performance evaluations. Moreover, written employee competencies foster transparency and consistency within the organization. Overall, the existence of explicit competencies for each position helps optimize organizational performance by ensuring that individuals possess the required skills and attributes to fulfill their roles competently.

Clarity

Clarifying the goals of an employee's job position and defining the specific actions required to achieve those goals are critical aspects of effective performance management. When employees clearly understand their job goals, they can align their efforts and prioritize their tasks accordingly. Clearly defined goals provide a sense of direction and purpose, helping employees stay focused and motivated. By breaking down the goals into specific actions, employees gain clarity on the steps they need to take to accomplish their objectives. This improves productivity and efficiency, as employees can eliminate ambiguity and streamline their workflows.

Key Performance Indicators (KPIs) and Standard Operating Procedures (SOPs) are pivotal in this process. KPIs are quantifiable metrics that measure an employee's performance and progress toward their goals. They provide tangible targets and benchmarks against which performance can be assessed. By having well-defined KPIs, employees clearly understand the expectations and can track their performance effectively.

SOPs, on the other hand, outline the standardized processes and procedures for each part of an employee's workflow. These documented instructions ensure consistency and quality in the execution of tasks. SOPs serve as references for employees, enabling them to follow best practices, minimize errors, and achieve optimal outcomes. They also facilitate knowledge sharing and seamless transitions between team members, as everyone can refer to the same guidelines.

KPIs and SOPs create a structured framework that promotes accountability, efficiency, and continuous improvement. They enable organizational leaders to monitor progress, identify areas for development, and provide necessary support or training to employees. Additionally, clearly defined goals, KPIs, and SOPs foster transparency and open communication, allowing for effective feedback and performance discussions. Ultimately, this clarity and structure contribute to the overall success of individuals and the organization.

Circumstance

When evaluating employee performance, it is important to consider the various circumstances that can impact their abilities and productivity, both within and outside the organization. These circumstances also referred to as setting events, encompass a range of factors that can significantly influence an employee's performance. Let's explore examples of potential circumstances that may impede employee performance:

1. Cultural: The customs, expectations, projections, and demographics within an organization can have a profound effect on employee performance. Different cultures may have distinct approaches to work, communication styles, and hierarchical structures. A lack of diversity within an organization can limit perspectives and hinder creativity. Recognizing and appreciating cultural differences is essential, fostering an inclusive environment that embraces diversity, as doing so can positively impact employee performance.

2. Situational: Situational factors, such as changes in workload, organizational restructuring, or external pressures, can significantly impact an employee's performance. For instance, if an employee is given an increased workload with or without adequate support or resources, it may lead to stress and decreased productivity. Evaluating performance without considering these situational factors would overlook crucial elements influencing an employee's performance.

3. Financial: Financial circumstances, both within and outside the organization, can significantly impact employee performance. Financial stressors, such as debt, low income, or unstable economic situations, can create distractions and affect an employee's focus and motivation. Recognition of financial challenges and providing appropriate support can contribute to improved performance and overall well-being.

4. Relational: Making workplace connections and establishing positive relationships is vital for an employee's performance. Misalignments in values, conflicts with colleagues or managers, or a lack of support can negatively impact motivation, collaboration, and job satisfaction. Recognizing the importance of positive work relationships and addressing relational issues by teaching employees to engage in emotionally safe conflict resolution practices can improve employee performance.

5. Emotional: Employee emotions, such as feelings of inadequacy, discomfort, or a lowered sense of belonging, can significantly influence their performance. Emotional well-being is critical in motivation, engagement, and job satisfaction. Organizations should foster a supportive and empathetic environment that encourages open communication and provides resources for managing stress and emotional challenges.

6. Functional: The functional circumstances of an employee, including their physical and mental health, can also impact their performance. Factors such as illness, general overwhelm, or neurodivergence can affect an individual's ability to perform at their best. Accommodations, flexibility, and support for employees facing functional challenges can optimize their performance and create a more inclusive work environment.

By acknowledging and addressing the various factors impacting an employee's performance, organizations can create a supportive and inclusive work environment that promotes growth, engagement, and overall success.

Culture

Company culture plays a significant role in shaping employee performance. It encompasses the values, norms, behaviors, and practices that define how things are done within an organization. When evaluating employee performance, leaders must consider the impact of company culture on individuals and their ability to perform at their best. Here are a few key aspects to consider:

1. Behavioral Contingencies: Company culture sets organizational behavior and performance standards. The behaviors and actions modeled, allowed, reinforced, or punished by leaders and colleagues profoundly influence employee performance. If a culture promotes transparency, accountability, and collaboration, it will likely foster high performance. Conversely, if negative behaviors or poor performance go unchecked or are even rewarded, it can create a detrimental work environment that negatively affects employee motivation and performance.

2. Distractions: A company culture allowing excessive distractions can hinder employee performance. Distractions can come in various forms, such as excessive meetings, inefficient communication channels, or a lack of focus on priorities. When evaluating employee performance, managers should consider the impact of such distractions on the employee's ability to concentrate, prioritize tasks, and maintain productivity. Addressing and minimizing distractions can significantly enhance performance and overall organizational effectiveness.

3. Poor Leadership: Leadership shapes company culture and employee performance. Poor leadership practices, such as micromanagement, lack of support or guidance, and inconsistent decision-making, can demotivate employees and hinder their performance. Evaluating employee performance should involve assessing leadership quality and identifying areas for improvement or support to enable better performance.

4. Alignment with Organizational Values: As discussed in previous chapters, when evaluating employee performance, it is essential to consider the alignment between an employee's values and those of the organization. If there is a misalignment, it can lead to a lack of motivation, disengagement, and underperformance. On the other hand, when an employee's values are aligned with the organization's mission and values, it can result in higher job satisfaction, commitment, and enhanced performance.

Considering company culture in performance evaluations promotes accuracy, accountability, and engagement. Company culture provides the context within which employees operate. Ignoring cultural influences would result in an incomplete understanding of the factors impacting employee performance. Evaluations that consider culture give a more accurate representation of an employee's capabilities and potential for growth.

Consequences

Leaders should be poised to implement consequences properly and fairly when addressing poor work performance. Consistency is of utmost importance, both ethically and legally, as it ensures fairness in the evaluation process. By establishing clear performance expectations and transparent consequences for not meeting them, organizations promote accountability and maintain a level playing field for all employees.

It is equally important to recognize and appreciate exemplary performance. Acknowledging and celebrating achievements boosts employee morale and motivation and reinforces a positive work culture. Honesty plays a key role in this process, as providing honest feedback, whether constructive criticism or recognition, is a form of kindness. Honest feedback allows employees to understand their strengths and areas for improvement, enabling their growth and professional development. Striking a balance between implementing consequences when necessary and recognizing and appreciating good performance promotes a healthy work environment and ultimately contributes to the organization's overall success.

Chapter 10:
Radical Joy
(A Memoir)

Joy is Our Birthright.

It won't benefit any of us if I beat around the bush in this chapter, so here we go:

My first 3 years in entrepreneurship did not fulfill me. And even as I write this, it feels like an act of courage to be so raw. Some days, I have even felt ungrateful. But if I am being 100% truthful, coming to terms with my own discontentment with what I had created has been perhaps the most freeing part of my journey thus far. And for you to understand why joy is essential, it's necessary to first address the things that robbed me of my joy in the first place.

First, I have never in my entire life seen a CEO be treated the way that I have been treated. And as much as I didn't want to pull the race card, especially in a company where more than 85% of my team is made up of people of color, it's my only explanation. Let me explain:

Someone (who I employed and whose opinion I trusted) told me that my actions were inconsistent with the organization's values. To be clear, I wrote those values. And the "actions" that this person indirectly referred to included me talking about race and sharing my stories about the experiences that shaped me as a leader and person on my *private* social media page. At first, I second-guessed my decision to be open about my journey. For the 50-11th time since we opened, I doubted myself as a leader.

→ *Am I hurting my team by telling the truth?*

→ *I'm certainly not talking about any of them or exposing anyone.*

→ *And also, who paid this person to correct me about what I do outside the workplace? To place me on a pedestal and then make her own determination about my worth? To define what leadership looks like in my own company?*

→ *And, more importantly, why was I so triggered by it?*

This wasn't a person of color, and she wasn't the first person to make a recommendation I did not ask for, particularly in this area. To my surprise, even people of color took issue with seeing a black woman in a position of power, and some of them were very clear about that in their actions toward me. And no matter how kind or accommodating of a leader

I was, or whether or not I gave them an actual seat at the table, it was never enough for them. And finally, I asked myself, *"Why are these people so distracted by me?"* And it became clear - the same reason that I had become distracted by them. The reason that I had chosen to keep the mission about Autism for all of this time. I was afraid that a mission for people of color wouldn't sit right with the global majority and that, as a result, I wouldn't have as big of an impact. So, with a vague mission statement, I called in people who wanted me to show up like their previous CEOs had shown up (if they had shown up at all). This image they had created in their minds of what a CEO looks like was more politically correct and, frankly, *less black.*

Internalized Racism

When people of color show characteristics of racism toward other people of color due to learned/systemic racism, it is often referred to as internalized racism or internalized oppression. Internalized racism occurs when individuals from marginalized racial or ethnic groups adopt and internalize negative stereotypes, prejudices, and discriminatory beliefs about their own group. This can lead to self-hatred, low self-esteem, and hostility towards others within their community.

Here are a few examples of internalized racism:

1. Colorism: Colorism is a form of discrimination based on the shade of one's skin tone within a racial or ethnic group. For

example, in some communities, lighter-skinned individuals might be perceived as more desirable or superior to those with darker skin, leading to bias and prejudice against darker-skinned individuals.

2. Racial Hierarchies: Internalized racism can manifest as adherence to racial hierarchies imposed by dominant groups. For instance, individuals might exhibit prejudice or discrimination based on ethnic backgrounds, language differences, or cultural practices within their own racial or ethnic group.

3. Cultural Assimilation: Some individuals may internalize racist beliefs and adopt the dominant culture's norms and values, rejecting or devaluing their cultural practices or traditions. This can stem from the pressure to conform to societal standards or gain acceptance within the dominant culture. *Hello! This is where I raise my hand and plead GUILTY!*

4. Stereotyping and Prejudice: Internalized racism can lead individuals to perpetuate stereotypes and prejudices against their own racial or ethnic group. This can manifest as biases related to intelligence, beauty, criminality, or other negative stereotypes perpetuated by systemic racism.

It is important to note that internalized racism is a consequence of systemic oppression and should not be viewed as an inherent characteristic

186

of individuals or communities. It results from the damaging effects of racism and discrimination, which can shape individuals' perceptions and behaviors.

If you understand that, you can understand why nobody, including myself, knew what it looked like for a black woman to have joy, especially in the workplace. So, instead of embracing the opportunity to finally pursue their happiness and safeguard their colleagues from reliving historical workplace trauma, they chose to deceive themselves and anyone else who would follow.

"She only cares about herself and her family" - as if everything shouldn't come second to those two things. I actually care about a lot of things. Especially people. *Especially marginalized people.*

"She's money-hungry" - because they weren't aware that every time I handed out a raise (which was every few weeks amid a recession), I chose to continue paying myself the bare minimum so that I didn't have to lay anyone off like the big companies were doing.

But also as if black women don't deserve wealth. I mean, certainly, in the land of the free, we all have the God-given right to start our own companies and obtain wealth for ourselves. But historically, empowered people want to acquire wealth for themselves at the expense of another person. It doesn't work that way, and that's where the disconnect is. Somewhere along the way, I may have indirectly made them feel this was possible.

There are several others:

"You exclude all other minorities here when you talk about black people."

"8% of our families are white. What if you rub them the wrong way?"

"The CEO needs to turn up her empathy."

"She told me that in her past, she has made people so uncomfortable that they would quit."

"I found out that Portia made my manager write me up, and that was my last straw."

"She was on the phone and didn't say hi to everyone when she came into the office."

And, (also a more iconic duo than Kendall + Kylie): *"Your hair looks very professional"* and *"Do black people actually experience microaggressions?"*

The worst part is that these statements cut so deep that I considered giving up multiple times. Not only because they weren't true but also because a part of me knew that they actually *believed themselves.* And that because of the color of my skin alone, if they told these fake, far-reaching ass stories to anyone else, they'd probably believe them. Certain people would be delighted to discover that the *real me* was too good to be true.

Booker T. Washington, an African-American educator, author, and leader, made his famous "crabs in a barrel" statement during his speech in 1901. The statement metaphorically describes the situation faced by

African-Americans in their struggle for progress and equality. In his remarks, Washington used the analogy of crabs in a barrel to depict a phenomenon he observed within the African-American community. He described how, when crabs are placed in a barrel, instead of working together to escape, they pull each other down in an attempt to climb out first. This behavior, he argued, hindered their collective progress and held them back from achieving success as a group.

By using the "crabs in a barrel" analogy, Washington aimed to highlight the destructive impact of internal divisions and competition within the African-American community. He argued that if African-Americans were to uplift themselves and advance as a race, they needed to support and assist each other rather than constantly struggle to surpass one another. By emphasizing cooperation and collaboration, Washington sought to inspire African-Americans to work together for their collective advancement.

Nonetheless, It wasn't any of these things that robbed me of my joy; My desire to fix them by changing how I showed up every day stripped me of my authenticity. So, after being asked to consider the one thing I want to be known for, I finally landed the plane. To clarify things for myself and my team, I changed my mission statement to align with my personal mission - *Equity*. And I know that that begins with creating safe spaces for people of color where we don't have to defend ourselves, explain ourselves, or diminish ourselves for being who we are. This goes for our team members, clients, and myself.

I chose to refocus and realized that the reason that I was triggered was because of the fact that I am a part of the community that I serve. To see me is to see my clients. The opposite is also true. This is why I spent 3 years feeling marginalized and brutally attacked in my own company and betrayed by my own people. And why it's even more critical that I stay the course. I once heard a woman say that working black people in America have to "cope with being black" on top of all the other pressures and stresses that being a part of the working class entails, and I thought, *"Jesus!"* It hurts to hear, but it is the absolute truth.

I learned that you can't code-switch your way into the good graces of others. And that if you ever want to have true fulfillment in those big shoes that God has placed on your feet, you need to be intentional. Get clear on your WHY. And if your own fulfillment is on that list, *even better.*

As for me - every morning when my feet hit the ground, I place one foot in front of the other and GO. *Unconditionally.* This is the takeaway of all takeaways for anyone who was born after about 1987 (wink).

My mission is to help other minority leaders reimagine themselves on the other side of whatever stunts their growth. To equip them with the essential skills, resilient systems, *and* mental fortitude that we *all* need to access and navigate our industries with precision, excellence, and all of the joy we deserve. And, if you need it, the permission to seek out that joy, if for no one else but yourself. We all deserve joy.

I experience joy when I can be fully present in my natural gifts and talents. And even when I don't feel particularly uplifted, I know God is doing the big things.

And I trust Him.

Credits.

Center for American Progress. (2021). According to the Center for American Progress, as of 2021, Black women held just 1.6% of executive or senior-level positions in S&P 500 companies. Retrieved from https://www.jpmorgan.com/insights/business/business-planning/black-women-are-the-fastest-growing-group-of-entrepreneurs-but-the-job-isnt-easy

Daniels, A. C. (2004). Performance management: Changing Behavior That Drives Organiztional Effectiveness. Performance Management Publications.

McKeown, G. (2014). Essentialism: The disciplined pursuit of less. Crown Business.

Morrison, T. (n.d.). The function, the very serious function of racism is a distraction. It keeps you from doing your work. It keeps you explaining, over and over again, your reason for being.

Russian Proverb. (n.d.). "If you chase two rabbits, you will not catch either one."

Washington, B. T. (1901). Address at the Cotton States and International Exposition, Atlanta, Georgia, September 18, 1901. Retrieved from [https://housedivided.dickinson.edu/sites/teagle/texts/booker-t-washington-up-from-slavery-1901/].

Williams DR, Lawrence JA, Davis BA. Racism and Health: Evidence and Needed Research. Annu Rev Public Health. 2019 Apr 1;40:105-125. Doi:

10.1146/annurev-publhealth-040218-043750. Epub 2019 Feb 2. PMID: 30601726; PMCID: PMC6532402.